Edited by Naomi Starkey | **May–August 2012**

The Bible Reading Fellowship
15 The Chambers, Vineyard, Abingdon OX14 3FE
Tel: 01865 319700; Fax: 01865 319701
E-mail: enquiries@brf.org.uk; Website: www.brf.org.uk

ISBN 978 1 84101 669 6

Distributed in Australia by Mediacom Education Inc., PO Box 610, Unley, SA 5061.
Tel: 1800 811 311; Fax: 08 8297 8719;
E-mail: admin@mediacom.org.au
Available also from all good Christian bookshops in Australia.
For individual and group subscriptions in Australia:
Mrs Rosemary Morrall, PO Box W35, Wanniassa, ACT 2903.

Distributed in New Zealand by Scripture Union Wholesale, PO Box 760, Wellington
Tel: 04 385 0421; Fax: 04 384 3990; E-mail: suwholesale@clear.net.nz

Publications distributed to more than 60 countries

Acknowledgments

Printed in Singapore by Craft Print International Ltd

Suggestions for using *New Daylight*

Find a regular time and place, if possible, where you can read and pray undisturbed. Before you begin, take time to be still and perhaps use the BRF prayer. Then read the Bible passage slowly (try reading it aloud if you find it over-familiar), followed by the comment. You can also use *New Daylight* for group study and discussion, if you prefer.

The prayer or point for reflection can be a starting point for your own meditation and prayer. Many people like to keep a journal to record their thoughts about a Bible passage and items for prayer. In *New Daylight* we also note the Sundays and some special festivals from the Church calendar, to keep in step with the Christian year.

New Daylight and the Bible

New Daylight contributors use a range of Bible versions, and you will find a list of the versions used opposite, on page 2. You are welcome to use your own preferred version alongside the passage printed in the notes, and this can be particularly helpful if the Bible text has been abridged.

New Daylight affirms that the whole of the Bible is God's revelation to us, and we should read, reflect on and learn from every part of both Old and New Testaments. Usually the printed comment presents a straightforward 'thought for the day', but sometimes it may also raise questions rather than simply providing answers, as we wrestle with some of the more difficult passages of Scripture.

New Daylight *is also available in a deluxe edition (larger format). Check out your local Christian bookshop or contact the BRF office, who can also give more details about a cassette version for the visually impaired. For a Braille edition, contact St John's Guild, 8 St Raphael's Court, Avenue Road, St Albans, AL1 3EH.*

Writers in this issue

David Winter is retired from parish ministry. An honorary Canon of Christ Church, Oxford, he is well known as a writer and broadcaster. His most recent book for BRF is *Facing the Darkness and Finding the Light*.

Naomi Starkey is a Commissioning Editor for BRF and edits and writes for *New Daylight* Bible reading notes. She has also written *Good Enough Mother* (BRF, 2009).

Rosie Ward was ordained in 1994, has served in three parishes and worked as a Leadership Development Adviser at CPAS. She has written several books, including *Growing Women Leaders* (BRF/CPAS, 2008).

Veronica Zundel is an Oxford graduate, writer and journalist. She lives with her husband and son in North London, where they belong to the Mennonite Church.

Stephen Rand is a writer and speaker who shares his time between Jubilee Debt Campaign, persecuted church charity Open Doors and Fresh Streams—a largely Baptist church leaders network.

Andrew Jones is Archdeacon of Meirionnydd in the Diocese of Bangor, rector of four churches on the Llyn Peninsula in North Wales, and an experienced pilgrimage leader. He has written *Pilgrimage* (BRF, 2011).

Tony Horsfall is a trainer and retreat leader with his own ministry, Charis Training. He is an elder of Ackworth Community Church and has written several books for BRF, including *Working from a Place of Rest*.

J. Stuart Weir has written *What the Book Says about Sport* (BRF, 2000), available as a download or in printed format from Verité Sport (www.veritesport.org).

Barbara Mosse, an Anglican priest, is currently a lecturer on the MA in Christian Spirituality at Sarum College, Salisbury. Her book *The Treasures of Darkness* was published by Canterbury Press in 2003.

John Proctor works for the URC, teaching New Testament in Cambridge and around the church. John has written *PBC Matthew* (BRF, 2001) and booklets on the Gospels and Acts in the Grove Biblical Series.

Helen Julian CSF is an Anglican Franciscan sister, currently serving her community as Minister Provincial. She has written three books for BRF, including *The Lindisfarne Icon* and *The Road to Emmaus*.

Naomi Starkey writes...

Welcome to what is probably a historic moment! In this issue we are trying something that, as far as I know, has not been tried before in New Daylight. We will be covering the whole Gospel of Mark over the next four months. No, we won't only be reading Mark (take a look at the Contents page to reassure yourself) and inevitably the contributors have had to be selective as to which bits of the Gospel to include, so you won't find the whole Bible text printed out here. The aim is to try to give more of a 'big picture' feel for this shortest and most fast-paced of the four Gospels, by covering as much of it as possible over two longer series of readings, lasting around three weeks each.

We continue with our mini-series on the themes of desert, exile and pilgrimage mentioned in my last editor's letter. This time, Andrew Jones considers exile, a key and catastrophic moment in the history of the Jewish people but also a theme that connects powerfully with our lives today. As he points out, 'If being "strangers in a strange land" defines exile, then, in many ways, we as Christians in the 21st century, in much of the Western world, are also in exile.' His 14 readings are both historically informative and spiritually thought-provoking.

We also begin another mini-series, taking a closer look at the lives of the three great patriarchs of the Old Testament, whose names recur so often in the phrase 'the God of Abraham, Isaac and Jacob'. We begin with Tony Horsfall and Abraham, focusing not so much on the familiar story as on what his life reveals about his relationship with God. Michael Mitton will be exploring the story of Isaac in our next issue.

And in case some of you had secretly hoped that *New Daylight* would be an Olympics-free zone—sorry! We couldn't let such a historic event pass without some mention of relevant themes. For a week in July, J. Stuart Weir of the charity Verité Sport is writing on 'God and the Olympics', with intriguing headings such as 'Did God create sport?' and 'Christian sports ethic'.

Naomi Starkey

The BRF Prayer

Almighty God,
you have taught us that your word is a lamp for our feet
and a light for our path. Help us, and all who prayerfully
read your word, to deepen our fellowship with each other
through your love. And in so doing may we come to know you more
fully, love you more truly, and follow more faithfully in
the steps of your son Jesus Christ, who lives and reigns with
you and the Holy Spirit, one God for evermore. Amen

Proverbs: wisdom for the world

Proverbs is unlike most of the other books in the Bible, but, conversely, it is very like a lot of ancient writings. It is a genre of writing known as 'Wisdom literature', which is practical advice, packaged in short, pithy sayings, often attached to a famous teacher—in this instance, Solomon.

Proverbs does not come in coherent passages, but in single wise sayings. Sometimes they seem to pick up a theme, but just as often they jump from topic to topic, like a flea on a molehill (just the sort of image its authors seem to love). To complicate things further, the translation is often obscure, the Hebrew and Greek versions contradicting each other.

On the other hand, these sayings are mostly intensely practical: they're about living well in the everyday world. They're about naughty children, over-sexed young men, nagging wives and lazy husbands. Some of this needs to be filtered through the long lens of history: we do not beat our children with rods, generally speaking, or regard most wives as nagging shrews. It is what we would call 'lifestyle counselling' and at times you may wonder why it is in the Bible at all, because God, faith and prayer do not feature in it very frequently.

Yet, when they do, they are what distinguishes Proverbs from other similar Wisdom literature from the ancient world. From time to time, Proverbs repeats its fundamental insight into the nature of wisdom: it springs from what it calls 'the fear of the Lord'—reverence for God and his holy Law. The 'Lord' here is Yahweh—the almighty and eternal God, the source of truth, knowledge, insight and judgment, all of which make up the biblical concept of wisdom. It is essentially the good and responsible life, lived in accordance with the will of God.

Proverbs sees wisdom as at the heart of everything. 'Wisdom' was a partaker in the very act of creation (Proverbs 8:22–31) and, at the end of the Bible's story, we find that Jesus, the Son of God, is Wisdom personified (1 Corinthians 1:24). As we read these 'wise sayings', it is important to set them in that context. Here are the nuts and bolts of everyday discipleship—but they spring from eternal sources.

David Winter

Tuesday 1 May

PROVERBS 27:1–6 (NRSV)

Boasting, folly, jealousy

Do not boast about tomorrow, for you do not know what a day may bring. Let another praise you, and not your own mouth—a stranger, and not your own lips. A stone is heavy, and sand is weighty, but a fool's provocation is heavier than both. Wrath is cruel, anger is overwhelming, but who is able to stand before jealousy? Better is open rebuke than hidden love. Well meant are the wounds a friend inflicts, but profuse are the kisses of an enemy.

Here are six wise sayings, with no apparent connection between them beyond their profound good sense. In the Sermon on the Mount, Jesus warned his followers against worrying about 'tomorrow'—that utterly unknown territory (Matthew 6:34). James also has trenchant advice for those who presume about the future: 'you do not even know what tomorrow will bring,' he says (James 4:13–15). Proverbs is certainly not advocating an irresponsible approach to future needs: the word 'boast' catches the note of danger. We must not take tomorrow, or next year, for granted.

Similarly, self-praise is no praise at all: let someone else speak it, if it is earned. To do otherwise is folly—and here we come across the chief target of Proverbs, the 'fool'. Folly and Wisdom are at loggerheads all through these sayings: they are moral opposites. The 'fool' in Proverbs is not someone who makes a mistake or looks ridiculous (that happens to all of us), but the person who thinks he knows better than his Creator.

The last of these sayings is a good example of Proverbs at its practical but profound best. 'Faithful are the wounds of a friend' is the KJV translation. When someone who genuinely loves us feels it necessary to speak words of rebuke or warning, it is an act of loyalty, not malice. Those who truly love us 'wound' us with words of caution or correction for our own good, not theirs. The 'enemy' can flatter away and then enjoy watching us make a mess of things.

Reflection

The greatest folly is to trust in our own wisdom. The greatest wisdom is sometimes to be found in the words of our friends.

DAVID WINTER

PROVERBS 27:7–11 (NRSV)

True friendship

The sated appetite spurns honey, but to a ravenous appetite even the bitter is sweet. Like a bird that strays from its nest is one who strays from home. Perfume and incense make the heart glad, but the soul is torn by trouble. Do not forsake your friend or the friend of your parent; do not go to the house of your kindred in the day of your calamity. Better is a neighbour who is nearby than kindred who are far away. Be wise, my child, and make my heart glad, so that I may answer whoever reproaches me.

They sound simple enough, but these five verses pose many problems of interpretation. It is usually safest to go for the most obvious reading, so verse 7 probably means little more than that hunger is the best sauce. At any rate, we all know how it feels to have eaten too much chocolate!

The straying bird in the next verse is rather different—the picture is of someone who has moved away from their secure place. We could apply it today to a youngster going off to university or an employee being sent by their firm to work in another country. Human beings have a great sense of 'place', which may be why Jesus promised to provide a 'place' for us beyond death (John 14:3). The Christian, of course, finds security not in geography but in relationship. We are 'in Christ'—a phrase that occurs again and again in some of Paul's letters in particular.

That also helps us with the rather elusive argument of the next few verses. What they seem to be saying is that when we are in times of trouble, we value most of all the support of our closest friends, especially if our relatives (family, kindred) are far away. Friendship is a great theme of Proverbs.

The last verse could be the prayer of any teacher or parent. If the child learns 'wisdom' (in the way Proverbs defines it) it will bring us credit, even if others prefer to criticise.

Reflection

'Some friends play at friendship but a true friend sticks closer than one's nearest kin' (Proverbs 18:24). What sort of a friend am I?

DAVID WINTER

PROVERBS 27:12, 14–17 (NRSV)

Practical wisdom

> The clever see danger and hide; but the simple go on, and suffer for it... Whoever blesses a neighbour with a loud voice, rising early in the morning, will be counted as cursing. A continual dripping on a rainy day and a contentious wife are alike; to restrain her is to restrain the wind or to grasp oil in the right hand. Iron sharpens iron, and one person sharpens the wits of another.

Taking the 'clever' as the 'wise' and the 'simple' as the 'foolish', the first verse states a sad but obvious truth. The wise see danger coming and take steps to avoid it. The foolish are oblivious of consequences and so suffer from them when they inevitably follow. It is important to remember again, however, what Proverbs means by wisdom and folly—the first is a gift from God; the second is thinking we know better than he does.

The noisy neighbour disturbing the peace of early morning with loud blessings may mean well, but those words or songs of praise may be an irritating or unwelcome disturbance to others. Perhaps there is a lesson here about choosing the right moment to speak out and the right moment to be silent.

The nagging wife is no stranger to the reader of Proverbs (see, for instance, 19:13). To avoid making this a sexism issue, perhaps we might simply say that the irritating and antisocial habits of any of us are not easily eradicated. (I love 'grasping oil in the hand'!) Once we are aware of them, it is obviously important to try, with God's help, to get rid of them. An important start, of course, is self-awareness, recognising the effect our behaviour is having on others—even our nearest and dearest. As for 'iron sharpening iron', can we see here a picture of the value of honest, open and frank argument? The apostles Peter and Paul managed to disagree without breaking fellowship (Galatians 2:11–14). Often we learn best when we are open to the ideas of others, even when we do not agree with them. To listen, even to those who oppose us, is not compromise but wisdom.

Reflection

Oh, to learn how to disagree without being disagreeable!

DAVID WINTER

PROVERBS 27:18–22 (NRSV)

The crucible of flattery

Anyone who tends a fig tree will eat its fruit, and anyone who takes care of a master will be honoured. Just as water reflects the face, so one human heart reflects another. Sheol and Abaddon are never satisfied, and human eyes are never satisfied. The crucible is for silver, and the furnace is for gold, so a person is tested by being praised. Crush a fool in a mortar with a pestle along with crushed grain, but the folly will not be driven out.

To 'take care' of a master is to serve him well. The reward for that is to be 'honoured'. Proverbs—in common with much of the Hebrew scriptures—sees virtue as earning earthly rewards, which was a natural enough position in times when there was no coherent belief in life beyond death. Like the owner of the fig tree, we can benefit from the fruit of our good work.

We can see our face in a pool of water and, it suggests here, we can see ourselves reflected in the hearts of those we know and love through the effect (good or bad) that we have on them.

Sheol and Abaddon are the abodes of the dead. Death is never sated—it always wants more—and so does the 'human eye': we see and we want. It is an idea picked up in one of John's letters in the New Testament, where he speaks of the 'desire of the eyes' (1 John 2:16). Discipline your 'looking'!

The notion of a crucible as a place of moral testing is a fairly common one in the Bible (see, for instance, 1 Peter 1:7). Here the fire that tests us is the hot flame of praise. How do we respond to it? Are we realistic enough to discern praise from flattery? Are we honest enough to appreciate criticism as well as praise?

The pestle, used for mixing medicines in a mortar, is another instrument of testing. Here, though, dealing with the fool who thinks himself wiser than God, the implication is gloomy indeed: 'The folly will not be driven out.'

Reflection

Thank God that Christ died for the sin of the world—
all of it, even that of the fool.

DAVID WINTER

PROVERBS 27:23–27 (NRSV)

Wise housekeeping

Know well the condition of your flocks, and give attention to your herds; for riches do not last for ever, nor a crown for all generations. When the grass is gone, and new growth appears, and the herbage of the mountains is gathered, the lambs will provide your clothing, and the goats the price of a field; there will be enough goats' milk for your food, for the food of your household and nourishment for your servant-girls.

You do not have to own lambs and goats, have servant-girls and live in a rural agricultural environment (which, we should remember, is the social setting of Proverbs) to know that earning a living and managing the housekeeping are important elements of life. Work, for most human beings, is not an optional extra but a necessity of life—and sometimes it is a chore, sometimes a pleasure.

There are two fundamental messages in this passage. The first is to recognise that possessions are transient. As Jesus said, the only treasure that lasts is the one we 'store up' in heaven (Matthew 6:20). Even royal wealth ('the crown') is passing. We cannot build our security on something that is temporary, whether it is next year's crop or money invested in stocks and shares.

Second, taking care, being responsible and fulfilling our obligations are all facets of godly wisdom. It is foolish to think that, if we neglect them, things will somehow nevertheless be all right. This is a point made trenchantly in the New Testament (see, for example, 1 Timothy 5:8, which describes anyone who does not provide for relatives as 'worse than an unbeliever').

There is, of course, another picture here. The very process by which rural life renews itself and provides for people's needs—sowing seeds, lambing, harvest—is a message of hope. Those who sow will reap. In Christian terms it is a model of renewal and resurrection.

Reflection

'Give us this day our daily bread' is a valid prayer, but the seeds must be sown, the harvest gathered in and the corn threshed to provide the flour. 'God gives life to the seed', but we have to plant it and gather its fruit.

DAVID WINTER

PROVERBS 28:1–5 (NRSV)

Understanding justice

The wicked flee when no one pursues, but the righteous are as bold as a lion. When a land rebels it has many rulers; but with an intelligent ruler there is lasting order. A ruler who oppresses the poor is a beating rain that leaves no food. Those who forsake the law praise the wicked, but those who keep the law struggle against them. The evil do not understand justice, but those who seek the Lord understand it completely.

In these verses we may need to look from time to time at alternative translations (you may well find them in footnotes at the bottom of the page in your Bible)—the meaning of several of them is uncertain. Verse 1 is clear enough, however: wicked people, it claims, lack courage—they even run away when there is no danger. On the other hand, 'the righteous' (that is, those who live by God's law) are as brave as lions.

The next two verses are about the use and abuse of worldly power. Once again, folly is the greatest handicap for a ruler—it is the wise ('intelligent') ruler who maintains security. To rebel against the divinely ordered rule was, in the ancient world, a recipe for disaster: Israel had nine kings in the two centuries leading up to 721BC and all but one of them came to power after an assassination. Then, in 721, the kingdom was conquered by Assyria.

I prefer the alternative reading of verse 3: 'A poor person who oppresses the poor'. There is something peculiarly evil about a person who forgets where they have come from and then oppresses the kind of people they once were: it is as unwelcome as unseasonal weather ('beating rain').

Probably the central message of these verses about social justice is found in verse 5. It is, as Proverbs constantly asserts, a matter of godly wisdom—'understanding'. The whole concept of justice is foreign to the thinking of the unwise, but those who turn to the Lord for wisdom will truly understand what it is.

Reflection

Disorder, oppression, moral cowardice are all the fruit of 'folly'.
The wisdom which is the 'fear of the Lord' is the answer.

DAVID WINTER

PROVERBS 28:6–10 (NRSV)

Walking in integrity

> Better to be poor and walk in integrity than to be crooked in one's ways even though rich. Those who keep the law are wise children, but companions of gluttons shame their parents. One who augments wealth by exorbitant interest gathers it for another who is kind to the poor. When one will not listen to the law, even one's prayers are an abomination. Those who mislead the upright into evil ways will fall into pits of their own making, but the blameless will have a goodly inheritance.

'Walking in integrity' pretty well sums up what it means to be a Christian—to walk 'in newness of life' (Romans 6:4). Here, of course, in the language of the Old Testament, it is the goal of the 'righteous', the 'wise', those who follow in God's commandments and so fulfil the 'whole duty of everyone' (Ecclesiastes 12:13).

The word 'integrity' conveys the idea of wholeness: elements that are integrated are brought together as one. The New Testament word for salvation also carries this sense of wholeness, being complete, at one with God, ourselves and our neighbour. To be 'saved' is to be spiritually healed—made whole. So to walk in integrity is to live an 'integrated' life—to become the 'joined-up' person God intends us to be.

The following verses amplify this in a series of examples. The life of integrity demands rigorous moral standards. It requires us to recognise fundamental moral absolutes. Godly poverty is better than ill-gotten riches. Gluttony is shameful in a world where many starve (as true then as it is now). Extortionate interest on loans (a great problem in the ancient world) destroys the lives of the borrowers and will, in the end, bring disgrace to the lender—again, a topical warning. Disobedience invalidates our prayers, because God requires honesty and truth. Those who lead good people astray will fall into their own deceitful pit.

'Walking' speaks of a measured, purposeful progress towards a goal. To walk in integrity is to proceed through life with God-given wisdom.

Reflection

'As you have therefore received Christ Jesus the Lord, continue to walk in him' (Colossians 2:6, literally).

DAVID WINTER

PROVERBS 28:11–16 (NRSV)

Appearances are deceptive

The rich is wise in self-esteem, but an intelligent poor person sees through the pose. When the righteous triumph, there is great glory, but when the wicked prevail, people go into hiding. No one who conceals transgressions will prosper, but one who confesses and forsakes them will obtain mercy. Happy is the one who is never without fear, but one who is hard-hearted will fall into calamity. Like a roaring lion or a charging bear is a wicked ruler over a poor people. A ruler who lacks understanding is a cruel oppressor; but one who hates unjust gain will enjoy a long life.

These sayings point up the difference between appearance and reality—the key word in verse 11 is 'pose'. Proverbs is much concerned with the problems and requirements of rulers—perhaps the king's ministers and courtiers were being warned of the danger of 'posing'. Honest self-examination is the remedy.

It is the wise—if poor—person who sees through the arrogance of the rich and powerful. It is the sinner who comes clean and confesses who obtains mercy, not the one who tries to cover up his or her deeds. It is not those who claim to be impervious to fear—the 'hard-hearted'—who find happiness, but those who are open to pain and suffering, their own or others'. A cruel and oppressive ruler may subjugate a whole nation, but he will not enjoy the long and happy life of the man who hates injustice.

These sayings express the same set of values as the Beatitudes (Matthew 5:1–11). They celebrate what we might call 'humble' virtues: meekness, mercy, purity of heart, righteousness. Each example also underlines a fundamental moral and biblical truth. Appearances are deceptive and, in practice, they do actually tend to deceive us. But God (and, hence, those who share his 'wisdom') is not deceived. His eye sees all and his judgment is sure.

Reflection

'Do not look on his appearance or on the height of his stature, because I have rejected him; for the Lord does not see as mortals see; they look on the outward appearance, but the Lord looks on the heart' (1 Samuel 16:7).

DAVID WINTER

PROVERBS 29:1–7 (NRSV)

A study in contrasts

> One who is often reproved, yet remains stubborn, will suddenly be broken beyond healing. When the righteous are in authority, the people rejoice; but when the wicked rule, the people groan. A child who loves wisdom makes a parent glad, but to keep company with prostitutes is to squander one's substance. By justice a king gives stability to the land, but one who makes heavy exactions ruins it. Whoever flatters a neighbour is spreading a net for the neighbour's feet. In the transgression of the evil there is a snare, but the righteous sing and rejoice. The righteous know the rights of the poor; the wicked have no such understanding.

The first impression we form of these sayings might be the reasonable one that they state the blindingly obvious. On a second look, however, we might notice that several of them touch deep chords of truth. For instance, the first verse speaks of the danger of the hardened heart—the 'stiff neck' of biblical imagery (see, for example, Exodus 34:9). There is, says the wise man, peril in ignoring warning signs and words of rebuke, because eventually we may become so immune to correction that our case is beyond redemption. Nearly 60 years ago, I heard the evangelist Billy Graham use this very verse to make the same point in relation to those who harden their hearts against the gospel.

At the level of daily living, the warning about flattery is shrewd. It may seem harmless to offer undeserved praise to friends, but it could turn their heads and expose them to ridicule or failure. To be valuable, a compliment needs to express the truth.

Equally, there is nothing obvious about the last of these sayings. The 'rights of the poor' are not self-evident. Historically the poor have simply been disregarded and their 'right' to a decent life ignored. The 'righteous' (those who seek to do what God requires), however, know that the poor also have God-given rights. They, too, are made in the image of God (Genesis 1:27) and are 'more valuable than many sparrows' (Matthew 10:31).

Reflection

Lord, soften my hard heart before it is broken beyond healing.

DAVID WINTER

Thursday 10 May

PROVERBS 29:11–15 (NRSV)

Justice and discipline

A fool gives full vent to anger, but the wise quietly holds it back. If a ruler listens to falsehood, all his officials will be wicked. The poor and the oppressor have this in common: the Lord gives light to the eyes of both. If a king judges the poor with equity, his throne will be established for ever. The rod and reproof give wisdom, but a mother is disgraced by a neglected child.

The best sort of control is self-control. Jesus makes the point in the Sermon on the Mount (see Matthew 5:22). To lose control—which is what anger really is—damages the angry person more than the object of their anger. So it is foolish to give way to anger and wise to control it. The notion of discipline is picked up again in Proverbs 29:15. 'The rod and reproof' feature quite a bit in Proverbs. In today's world, we choose other instruments of discipline where children are concerned—withholding treats, limiting outings and so on—rather than corporal punishment. Having said this, few parents would deny that children need boundaries and sanctions to enforce them sometimes. To fail to provide those boundaries is, says the wise man, 'neglect'.

The other sayings have to do with the use and abuse of power. The king must judge the poor with fairness if he wishes to preside over a stable kingdom. In the process, he will need to discern what is true and what is false or his whole government will be corrupted. Essentially, all power lies exposed to the eye of God. He searches the hearts of both the oppressor and the oppressed—a sobering thought. He also understands the plight of those who are oppressed and knows both the motivation and the methods of the oppressor. Mercy and justice are two essential elements of the wisdom of God, and both will be at work in any situation of exploitation or oppression.

Reflection

'Your rod and your staff, they comfort me' (Psalm 23:4). The rod and staff, both instruments of 'discipline', were there to make the sheep's life better, not the shepherd's.

DAVID WINTER

PROVERBS 29:17–20, 22 (NRSV)

The transforming vision

Discipline your children, and they will give you rest; they will give delight to your heart. Where there is no prophecy, the people cast off restraint, but happy are those who keep the law. By mere words servants are not disciplined, for though they understand, they will not give heed. Do you see someone who is hasty in speech? There is more hope for a fool than for anyone like that... One given to anger stirs up strife, and the hothead causes much transgression.

The theme of discipline continues—and not just of children. 'Servants'—which means slaves—also need to be controlled (not a problem for most of us nowadays), but so do those who cannot control what they say. Those who blurt out things, sometimes justifying it by boasting 'I speak my mind', are worse than fools, presumably because they can do more harm. How often are friendships broken, churches split, families divided by words hastily spoken? James is very strong on the need to control our 'unruly' tongues (3:9). Similarly the one 'given to anger' is a menace—this is not the person who once in a while loses his temper, but a person who is habitually prone to outbursts of anger. Like God himself, we are to be 'slow to anger' (Psalm 103:8).

The key verse, of course, is Proverbs 29:18. 'Prophecy' is divine revelation: what God wants us to know in any given situation. There were times in the history of Israel when this prophetic voice was absent and the people were starved of the truth (1 Samuel 3:1). The well-known KJV translation of this verse, instead of 'prophecy', has 'vision', which implies that we have to 'see' something, have a greater goal, but, in fact, the opposite is the truth. The 'people' cast off restraint when they are either unaware that God has spoken or choose to ignore what he has said. Prophecy, in this sense, is indeed 'the word of God'. That 'word' might be in the Bible or come to us from human lips or even our own private reflection. We ignore it at our peril.

Reflection

How, in our present situation, can people (including myself) 'hear' the prophetic voice of God?

DAVID WINTER

Divine justice

A person's pride will bring humiliation, but one who is lowly in spirit will obtain honour. To be a partner of a thief is to hate one's own life; one hears the victim's curse, but discloses nothing. The fear of others lays a snare, but one who trusts in the Lord is secure. Many seek the favour of a ruler, but it is from the Lord that one gets justice. The unjust are an abomination to the righteous, but the upright are an abomination to the wicked.

Yet again we have an apparently random selection of wise sayings, yet (as with so much of Proverbs) there is an underlying unity to them. Notice the contrasting values: pride, lowly; thief, victim; fear, trust; favour, justice; wicked, righteous. The whole message of the book is there, because the 'wise' (the discerning, the God-fearing) are able to distinguish between those who are good and those who are bad, to recognise the spiritual danger signals. The 'fool', on the other hand, fails to see the difference and pays the price of his folly.

What is a Christian—a child of the new covenant—to make of Proverbs? Much of it is echoed in the moral teaching of the Gospels and the epistles of the New Testament. There is plenty in the Sermon on the Mount, for instance, that deals with exactly these values. Meekness, humility, righteousness and trust are all there. So, on the negative side, are pride, arrogance, injustice, anger and folly.

As mentioned in the Introduction, the key to Proverbs is: 'the fear of the Lord is the beginning of wisdom' (9:10; 15:33). 'Fear', in this sense, is not abject terror, but reverence, which is shown by a genuine desire to do what God requires. Jesus said, 'Blessed are those who hunger and thirst for righteousness' (Matthew 5:6). That is true worship. Perhaps the great 'extra' of the Christian revelation is its emphasis on grace, because if we are truly to find that righteousness, it will be when we see it as a gift of God.

Reflection

It is a wonderful truth that one gets justice from the Lord. It is an equally wonderful truth that he is the source of mercy.

DAVID WINTER

The absence of God

When we think of 'the absence of God', we probably turn to those times when we have struggled to believe, when 'God' has seemed a distant concept rather than a present and personal reality. An overwhelming sense of God's absence—the 'dark night of the soul', to use a classic spiritual phrase—can be a vivid and painful experience for many. At the same time, it is not beyond the bounds of possibility that sometimes we, and sometimes even our church communities, can end up obscuring rather than enhancing an awareness of God's presence for others.

The next two weeks of readings are patterned as follows. In the days leading up to Ascension (17 May), we shall take a brief walk through the events of the death, burial and resurrection of Jesus, touching on what they can reveal to us about coping with God's apparent absence. Following Ascension Day itself, we shall go on to explore some of the implications, which relate in part to our responsibility as Christians to witness to what we know and believe about God's presence with us, however dark life's circumstances. These implications also point to how we can cling to the fundamental truth that God is indeed with us, Emmanuel, no matter how lonely, broken or lost we may feel.

As I have worked on these notes, I have found it fascinating to bring together the idea of God's absence with Ascension—a day in the Church's year that can be overlooked in many churches. Might that be because this event is one we struggle to classify? Is it actually an event to celebrate or in some way mourn? A word that has kept returning to me is 'poignant'—something not easily identifiable as 'happy' *or* 'sad', but still involving an intensity of emotion that can pierce the heart. The Lord *is* here, his Spirit *is* with us—and yet we cannot touch his arm or lean against him, as his friends once touched and leaned. Like them, however, we shall learn to love him with a love that is strong, deep and true, yet is also about releasing to the world, rather than jealously possessing, the Beloved.

Naomi Starkey

PSALM 22:1–6, 19 (NRSV)

The cry from the cross

My God, my God, why have you forsaken me? Why are you so far from helping me, from the words of my groaning? O my God, I cry by day, but you do not answer; and by night, but find no rest. Yet you are holy, enthroned on the praises of Israel. In you our ancestors trusted; they trusted, and you delivered them. To you they cried, and were saved; in you they trusted, and were not put to shame. But I am a worm, and not human; scorned by others, and despised by the people… But you, O Lord, do not be far away! O my help, come quickly to my aid!

Naked, bloodied, shuddering with cold after three hours of darkness, hanging in torment at the Place of the Skull, Jesus cries out 'with a loud voice' (Mark 15:34) the opening words of this psalm. Dare we paraphrase it as 'screamed'—or does that disturb too much our belief in an omnipotent, omniscient, eternal Saviour?

One of the earliest heresies of the Church was Docetism, from the Greek *doceo*, to seem. Its proponents contended that Jesus only took on the *appearance* of humanity, because how could the immortal become mortal? Even today we can struggle to remember the humanity of Christ, forgetting that—as the writer to the Hebrews tells us—he is one 'who in every respect has been tested as we are' (4:15).

That cry of Jesus speaks of intense, undeniable humanity. Although he knew he was the Son of God, he could not 'rise above the situation' and 'simply believe', but felt abandoned by the one he called Father. What a comfort that can be to all those who have ever felt guilty for such a response to a difficult situation!

Wonderfully, Psalm 22, like so many other psalms, starts in despair but finishes with words of renewed confidence, even joy. Jesus chose to voice his despair with an ancient prayer that returns, in the end, to affirm that God is good; when we fear we are falling for ever, he is there to catch us.

Reflection

'He did not hide his face from me, but heard when I cried to him' (Psalm 22:24).

NAOMI STARKEY

Monday 14 May

LUKE 23:50–56 (NRSV, ABRIDGED)

Dead and gone

> Now there was a good and righteous man named Joseph... and he was waiting expectantly for the kingdom of God. This man went to Pilate and asked for the body of Jesus. Then he took it down, wrapped it in a linen cloth, and laid it in a rock-hewn tomb where no one had ever been laid... The women who had come with [Jesus] from Galilee followed, and they saw the tomb and how his body was laid. Then they returned, and prepared spices and ointments. On the sabbath they rested according to the commandment.

When somebody is martyred, their dead body has special significance for their friends and followers—hence the lengths to which their executioners will go to deny them any part of that body and the veneration accorded to 'religious' relics—a single fingerbone, a phial of blood, a lock of hair. If that makes us feel a bit prickly and Protestant, try browsing the Internet to see how much value can be placed on 'secular' relics—a signed photograph, a used serviette, a rock star's unwashed T shirt...

We can only guess at the crushing desolation of Jesus' disciples on that sabbath eve. If he had been who he had claimed to be—the Son of God—was God now dead? Were they facing not only the loss of their master but also the loss of the faith that had sustained their people for so long? If they could not bring themselves to believe that, the unavoidable conclusion was that Jesus had been deluded. Inspirational, possessed of extraordinary powers, but deluded—and with them no longer.

Matthew tells us (27:55) that the women mentioned here had accompanied Jesus from back home in Galilee to look after him. There seemed nothing left for them to do now except prepare for a final, intimate act of care. Surely many tears were shed as those spices and ointments were prepared—but I imagine that some of their tears would have arisen from anger and a sense of betrayal as well of love.

Prayer

Thank you, almighty God, that you are bigger than all the anger, pain and loss that we could ever feel. May we remember that and find security in the remembering.

NAOMI STARKEY

JOHN 20:11–14 (NRSV)

Beyond imagining

Mary stood weeping outside the tomb. As she wept, she bent over to look into the tomb; and she saw two angels in white, sitting where the body of Jesus had been lying, one at the head and the other at the feet. They said to her, 'Woman, why are you weeping?' She said to them, 'They have taken away my Lord, and I do not know where they have laid him.' When she had said this, she turned round and saw Jesus standing there, but she did not know that it was Jesus.

In our Easter celebrations, we can overlook the fact that the first resurrection morning began with even bleaker emotions than those that had dominated the previous days. Jesus' body had disappeared. There was nothing left to touch, no focus for mourning, no physical reminder of those brief but breathtaking years of Jesus' ministry.

We may be tempted to rush on to the next verses of the story, about which Margaret Silf wrote so movingly for Holy Week this year—when Mary recognises Jesus as he speaks her name. It is poignant, however, to pause at this desolate moment, even as the final sentence of our reading trembles with the glorious miracle to trump all miracles. Maybe Jesus' friends had to face losing their very last reminder of his earthly presence before they could receive what God had in store for them instead: something beyond imagining.

Jesus had a new, resurrection body whereby he was identifiably himself—but not at first glance. He was in some way different, such that even those who knew him struggled to recognise him at first. His familiar and much-loved mortal body was transformed in a foreshadowing of the transformation promised to every child of his Father, every one of us. God's transforming love is at work within our hearts even now, shaping us into the sons and daughters he has always longed for us to be. One day, in his presence, that inner transformation will be fully visible when we, too, are blessed with the healed and heavenly bodies of resurrected life.

Prayer

O God of Easter morning, give us the courage to hold our hands and hearts open to all that you would give us.

NAOMI STARKEY

Luke 24:28–32 (NRSV)

Stay with us

As [the two disciples] came near the village to which they were going, [Jesus] walked ahead as if he were going on. But they urged him strongly, saying, 'Stay with us, because it is almost evening and the day is now nearly over.' So he went in to stay with them. When he was at the table with them, he took bread, blessed and broke it, and gave it to them. Then their eyes were opened, and they recognised him; and he vanished from their sight. They said to each other, 'Were not our hearts burning within us while he was talking to us on the road, while he was opening the scriptures to us?'

I find this one of the most endearing of the resurrection appearances because of its homeliness. Two people are walking sadly home after that terrible Friday in Jerusalem. Jesus comes alongside them, unrecognised, and begins to explain the significance of what has been happening. When they reach their destination, Jesus seems about to walk on into the night, but is persuaded to join them for supper and more conversation. Their new friend prays a blessing on the bread and breaks it—just as he did at the Passover supper before he died—and it is then that they know him, whereupon he vanishes.

There it is again, that note of poignancy. Jesus is alive again, but in a different way. He is there, but then he is not. They cannot hold on to him; they have to accept his presence not as a special favour limited to his closest friends, but as a gift to empower them to share abroad the astonishingly good news of the kingdom.

We may fear that we will never be brave or strong enough to make use of such a gift. Indeed, our present circumstances may speak to us only of divine absence or indifference rather than presence. The story of that encounter on the Emmaus road can give us hope, though, that even if our days feel like a dreary trudge, we do not trudge alone.

Prayer

Risen Jesus, open our eyes to see you walking with us as we continue our journey through the lives with which we have been blessed.

Naomi Starkey

LUKE 24:46–52 (NRSV)

Returning with great joy

[Jesus] said to [his followers], 'Thus it is written, that the Messiah is to suffer and to rise from the dead on the third day, and that repentance and forgiveness of sins is to be proclaimed in his name to all nations, beginning from Jerusalem. You are witnesses of these things. And see, I am sending upon you what my Father promised; so stay here in the city until you have been clothed with power from on high.' Then he led them out as far as Bethany, and, lifting up his hands, he blessed them. While he was blessing them, he withdrew from them and was carried up into heaven. And they worshipped him, and returned to Jerusalem with great joy.

This is the first of Luke's two accounts of the ascension. While the second (Acts 1) places more emphasis on the developing mission of the Church, here we are left with scenes of blessing and 'great joy' (v. 52). Jesus returns to his Father and his followers must wait for the exciting and mysterious 'power from on high' (v. 49).

To me, there is poignancy in the mention of Bethany, where Jesus' dear friends Mary, Martha and Lazarus lived. It was where he had probably been at his most relaxed, a place where he could rest, eat, laugh, cry. What would we not give to have the privilege of knowing the earthly Jesus as closely as that? Yet that relationship had to end, as all such relationships end—through death—and then an infinitely deeper one could develop, which would transform every one of Jesus' followers and, through them, the world.

Both my brothers cried for days when they started school, but eventually found the courage to let go of our mother willingly. They realised that, although they could not see her for a time, she had not vanished forever. It was the next stage of their growing up. Ascension Day—when, in one sense, the world 'lost' Jesus—points us to Pentecost and the gift of the Holy Spirit to the infant Church, bringing courage, love and, most significantly, the energy to continue the process of growing to maturity.

Reflection

'I will not leave you orphaned; I am coming to you' (John 14:18).

NAOMI STARKEY

Colossians 1:15–20 (NRSV)

Making visible the invisible

He is the image of the invisible God, the firstborn of all creation; for in him all things in heaven and on earth were created, things visible and invisible, whether thrones or dominions or rulers or powers—all things have been created through him and for him. He himself is before all things, and in him all things hold together. He is the head of the body, the church; he is the beginning, the firstborn from the dead, so that he might come to have first place in everything. For in him all the fullness of God was pleased to dwell, and through him God was pleased to reconcile to himself all things, whether on earth or in heaven, by making peace through the blood of his cross.

The challenge of this first week of readings is becoming clear: Jesus died, rose, ascended and sent his Spirit. Therefore, it is now the responsibility of 'the body'—his body, which is the Church—to point out to the watching, questioning world that here is the way, the truth and the life (see John 14:6). Over the following days, we shall reflect on how the Church executes that task—and some of the consequences when it fails to do so.

Today's passage reminds us that, in one sense, God is forever 'absent'. In other words, he is not present in the physical universe in the same way as are we, his creatures. A major part of the sorry history of humanity is our endless striving to generate 'God' in tangible form, something to grasp and shape to our liking (see 20 May for more on this). We worship an 'invisible God', but, crucially, we see his exact likeness in his Son, Jesus.

When people demand of us, 'What is your God like?', we can point them to the story of Jesus, as found in scripture. We can also share with them, humbly and hesitantly, whatever experiences we may have had of the love and power of the risen Jesus. Thus, we play our own small part in making the invisible visible.

Prayer

Living Lord, in your mercy use us as your agents of reconciliation.

Naomi Starkey

JEREMIAH 2:5–8 (NRSV, ABRIDGED)

Always forgetting

Thus says the Lord: What wrong did your ancestors find in me that they went far from me, and went after worthless things, and became worthless themselves? They did not say, 'Where is the Lord who brought us up from the land of Egypt, who led us in the wilderness...?' I brought you into a plentiful land to eat its fruits and its good things. But when you entered you defiled my land, and made my heritage an abomination. The priests did not say, 'Where is the Lord?' Those who handle the law did not know me; the rulers transgressed against me; the prophets prophesied by Baal, and went after things that do not profit.

I mentioned yesterday the 'sorry history of humanity'. Today, we plunge back centuries to the time of Jeremiah to remember just how repetitive that history has been. We may lament the state of the Church today, but, back then, the 'body' intended as a witness to the Lord Almighty—the nation of Israel—was in desperate straits.

The prophet expresses God's anguish: how could his people forget all that he had done for them? Israel had been chosen for a covenant with the Lord to fulfil the promise to Abraham that, through him, 'all the families of the earth shall be blessed' (Genesis 12:3). Even though God had done his full share of delivering and blessing, his people 'went after worthless things' (Jeremiah 2:5).

This is not so much a case of 'the absence of God' as 'the flight from God'. God is absent because the people have done their utmost to absent themselves from him. Before we condemn, though, we should consider whether we are consciously drawing closer to God's presence or actually trying to escape in some way. For example, do we heed the promptings of conscience—that God-given inner thermostat that warns of spiritual chill—or are we as wilfully disobedient as the long-ago Israelites?

Reflection

'See, the Lord's hand is not too short to save, nor his ear too dull to hear. Rather, your iniquities have been barriers between you and your God, and your sins have hidden his face from you so that he does not hear' (Isaiah 59:1–2).

NAOMI STARKEY

ISAIAH 44:14B–17 (NRSV)

A personal god

> [The carpenter] plants a cedar and the rain nourishes it. Then it can be used as fuel. Part of it he takes and warms himself; he kindles a fire and bakes bread. Then he makes a god and worships it, makes it a carved image and bows down before it. Half of it he burns in the fire; over this he roasts meat, eats it, and is satisfied. He also warms himself and says, 'Ah, I am warm, I can feel the fire!' The rest of it he makes into a god, his idol, bows down to it, and worships it; he prays to it and says, 'Save me, for you are my god!'

I grew up reading missionary stories (my grandparents spent most of their lives in such work) and was fascinated by the idea that many people around the world devoted themselves to 'idol worship'—offering sacrifices (chickens were popular) to scary statues. Over the following years, I heard plenty of sermons pointing out how celebrities, possessions, careers, even friends, can become idols, taking God's place in our hearts.

Being mindful of this, it is still easy to create a false God for ourselves, formed of assumptions, prejudices and half-truths. We shape him to suit our circumstances and worship him, Sunday by Sunday, and, when life does not turn out as we expect, we may turn on this God angrily: 'Why have you let us down? Didn't we say the right words, do the right things?' In our anger, we may think we are facing up to God's absence, but we actually may have to admit that we did not connect with the true God in the first place.

Some would argue for the usefulness of the Anglican image of a three-legged stool to explain how to understand our faith—the three legs comprising scripture, church tradition and human reason. As we seek to discover more of the true God, this image is a helpful corrective to today's tendency to make things up as we go along, guided by our feelings and, perhaps, the latest Christian teaching from across the Atlantic…

Prayer

God of Abraham, Isaac and Jacob, Father God of all,
grant us a little glimpse of who you truly are.

NAOMI STARKEY

EZEKIEL 34:2B, 4, 10 (NRSV, ABRIDGED)

Not doing the job

Thus says the Lord God: Ah, you shepherds of Israel who have been feeding yourselves! Should not shepherds feed the sheep?... You have not strengthened the weak, you have not healed the sick, you have not bound up the injured, you have not brought back the strayed, you have not sought the lost, but with force and harshness you have ruled them... Thus says the Lord God, I am against the shepherds; and I will demand my sheep at their hand... I will rescue my sheep from their mouths, so that they may not be food for them.

Here Ezekiel is speaking to those who should have been the godly leaders—the shepherds—of Israel, but were woefully failing in their task. The image of God as shepherd of his people is a familiar one from scripture, but the actual shepherding task was delegated to the ones selected and anointed to be his hands and feet on earth.

It is tempting to read this passage and allow ourselves a little self-satisfied glow as we contemplate the failures of others. The glow might start to fade if we consider exactly how much *we* have 'strengthened the weak, healed the sick, sought the lost' and so on. As disciples of Jesus, we all have some share in that responsibility, even if we do not lead a church or hold public office. Others tend to judge the Christian faith by the words and deeds of its adherents. What they may see is selfishness, unkindness, arrogance and ongoing battles over various ethical debates that, frankly, are of secondary importance at best when it comes to proclaiming the gospel message.

Those of us who have the daunting privilege of leadership should remember that kindness, rather than perfectly correct doctrine, is what may well speak loudest to those outside the Church, The rest of us should pray for our leaders and, where appropriate, remind them of the importance of caring for their flock rather than simply grandstanding on 'issues'.

Reflection

Jesus said, 'I am the good shepherd. The good shepherd lays down his life for his sheep' (John 10:11). What might this mean in practice for those called to lead God's people today?

NAOMI STARKEY

PSALM 10:1–4, 11 (NRSV)

God at a distance

Why, O Lord, do you stand far off? Why do you hide yourself in times of trouble? In arrogance the wicked persecute the poor—let them be caught in the schemes they have devised. For the wicked boast of the desires of their heart, those greedy for gain curse and renounce the Lord. In the pride of their countenance the wicked say, 'God will not seek it out'; all their thoughts are, 'There is no God.'... They think in their heart, 'God has forgotten, he has hidden his face, he will never see it.'

Sebastian Faulks' novel *A Week in December* includes one of the most chilling characters in recent fiction. John Veals is a man for whom adjectives such as 'manipulative', 'calculating' and 'ruthless' barely begin to do justice. He is an enormously successful, utterly unscrupulous city financier who, with a few phone calls, can close deals resulting in ruin for whole countries. He becomes even wealthier; the poor are crushed.

The psalmist despairs at God's absence in the face of deliberate wickedness (as opposed to natural disasters, such as earthquakes and tsunamis, which are not a direct consequence of human behaviour). It is less a case of 'Is there a God?' than 'Why is he keeping such a low profile?' After all, if (as many believe) God still intervenes today to heal, give prophetic words, touch individual lives, why can he not take direct action to stop evil people doing their worst?

The inescapable answer is 'free will'. Humanity has the God-given capability to choose and, although we often make good choices, there are too many times when our choices lead to harm. If we seek to live as God's children, our calling is to do all we can to remind the world—and the church—of the values of God's kingdom as found throughout scripture: caring for the poor, working for equitable economic systems, protecting the environment, revealing God's love to others. God is not hiding; he is waiting for us to take action.

Reflection

These may be familiar words, but they remain powerfully true: 'The only thing necessary for the triumph of evil is for good men to do nothing' (attributed to Edmund Burke, 1729–97).

NAOMI STARKEY

JOHN 11:32–37 (NRSV)

The last hope

When Mary came where Jesus was and saw him, she knelt at his feet and said to him, 'Lord, if you had been here, my brother would not have died.' When Jesus saw her weeping, and the Jews who came with her also weeping, he was greatly disturbed in spirit and deeply moved. He said, 'Where have you laid him?' They said to him, 'Lord, come and see.' Jesus began to weep. So the Jews said, 'See how he loved him!' But some of them said, 'Could not he who opened the eyes of the blind man have kept this man from dying?'

In contrast to the last two readings, in this passage we see the point beyond which no human action is of any use. Mary's brother is dead. The Son of God failed to turn up and, when he finally does come, it is seemingly too late for anything except bitter tears. Even today, in an era of extraordinary medical advances, the moment always comes when death is inevitable, when earthly help is exhausted. We turn to prayer, which may have been our first hope but is also surely always our last... and the answer seems to be either negative or just silence.

The pain is unspeakable—and close on the heels of pain comes anger. Even as Jesus shakes with grief at the loss of Lazarus, some of those watching respond with anger. He could have made a difference; he did not; he obviously did not care so very much.

Jesus' passionate response to the horror of death is to bring his friend back to life, showing that the kingdom of heaven is unstoppable and offering a foretaste of the future resurrection promised to all. In the light of this miracle and (even more so) his own resurrection life, we need not fear being cut off from God by the grave. Knowing this, though, we must still wait for the full consequences to unfold. As we live in this in-between time, we have to trust that the Father's love is strong and real enough to hold us in our tear-streaked misery.

Reflection

'You have kept count of my tossings; put my tears in your bottle' (Psalm 56:8).

NAOMI STARKEY

PSALM 130 (NRSV)

Waiting for the Lord

Out of the depths I cry to you, O Lord. Lord, hear my voice! Let your ears be attentive to the voice of my supplications! If you, O Lord, should mark iniquities, Lord, who could stand? But there is forgiveness with you, so that you may be revered. I wait for the Lord, my soul waits, and in his word I hope; my soul waits for the Lord more than those who watch for the morning, more than those who watch for the morning. O Israel, hope in the Lord! For with the Lord there is steadfast love, and with him is great power to redeem. It is he who will redeem Israel from all its iniquities.

Here we find despair at God's absence mingled with hope. The psalmist calls from 'the depths' (v. 1)—by contrast with Psalm 139, he does not seem able to sense the presence of the Lord with him in that place of terror and turmoil.

A child secure in the knowledge that they are loved has a pretty much unshakeable confidence that if they cry out in fear in the night, somebody will come and comfort them. This does not make their fear any less real and their crying may still be desperate, but the certainty of consolation sustains them, even as they listen out for the footsteps on the stairs.

We might hazard a guess from the psalmist's mention of 'iniquities' and 'forgiveness' that he ended up in the depths as a result of his own actions. He feels far from God's presence, floundering in darkness, but still has enough strength to hold on to what he knows to be true: the Lord is both loving and redeeming, not only to individuals but also whole nations, even when they have done wrong. Despite the gulf between himself and God, he refuses to give up hope. As surely as the sun rises, so he knows that, in the end, he will be saved.

Reflection

'I believe that I shall see the goodness of the Lord in the land of the living.
Wait for the Lord; be strong, and let your heart take courage;
wait for the Lord!' (Psalm 27:13–14).

NAOMI STARKEY

ROMANS 8:18, 22–25 (NRSV)

Hidden glory

I consider that the sufferings of this present time are not worth comparing with the glory about to be revealed to us... We know that the whole creation has been groaning in labour pains until now; and not only the creation, but we ourselves, who have the first fruits of the Spirit, groan inwardly while we wait for adoption, the redemption of our bodies. For in hope we were saved. Now hope that is seen is not hope. For who hopes for what is seen? But if we hope for what we do not see, we wait for it with patience.

Reading this passage, we should remember that, in referring to labour pains, Paul is not thinking of the sort of groans associated with waking and stretching in the morning. Nor is he talking about waiting as a kind of 'Ho hum, this is taking a while' feeling. He meant to evoke a kind of intense pain that overwhelms all thought, all perspective and any awareness that it will come to an end.

We are waiting for the completion of God's work of salvation, the full realisation of the resurrection hope of Easter and the final outworking of the promise of Pentecost. As we saw on Wednesday, this in-between time can be dominated by pain, suffering and loss, but it is also suffused with hope. In God's good time, we hope that everything will be brought to completion; we will see him face to face; his glory will be visible to every eye. As Jesus pointed out, when a baby is born, the pain of giving birth is forgotten (John 16:21). When our redemption is complete, the ache and longing that may fill our hearts now will shrink to nothing.

Meanwhile, as we groan and wait and try to be patient, we can join with God's work in the world, doing faithfully and obediently whatever is given us to do. We may fear we will never see the end result, the pay-off for our efforts, but that is why both hope and patience are so vital for our ongoing journey through life.

Prayer

Lord God, grant us not only your transcendent peace
but also a measure of your infinite patience.

NAOMI STARKEY

1 KINGS 8:10–13 (NRSV)

Into the darkness

And when the priests came out of the holy place, a cloud filled the house of the Lord, so that the priests could not stand to minister because of the cloud; for the glory of the Lord filled the house of the Lord. Then Solomon said, 'The Lord has said that he would dwell in thick darkness. I have built you an exalted house, a place for you to dwell in for ever.'

Our final reading comes from the dedication of Solomon's temple. After the ark of the covenant had been installed in the most 'holy place' (v. 10) and the priests had withdrawn, the cloud of God's glory filled the place. A footnote in the NRSV links Solomon's words to Psalm 97, where God is described as surrounded by swirling cloud, darkness and lightning, just as at Sinai when the Law was first given to Moses.

All such descriptions are, in the end, fumbling attempts to use human language and earthly imagery to express the inexpressible and describe the indescribable. Over the centuries, many Christians have come to a point where they feel it is easier to try and grasp something of God by defining what he is not, rather than what he is. Known as the *via negativa*, or 'negative way', this has been a stronger emphasis in Eastern Christian traditions, especially the Orthodox Church.

Yes, of course, we believe that we find God in scripture and the Church and supremely revealed in Jesus Christ, but we can never hope to encompass the eternal with our finite minds. Instead, we can dare to step out into the darkness, beyond the borders of knowledge and understanding and what we think we know about God. We can dare to venture deeper and deeper into his presence, willing to hold open our hands to whatever he will give us, admitting our emptiness so that his Spirit can truly fill us, remembering that his apparent absence is simply the shadow cast by his immense and unavoidable presence.

Reflection

'I will give you the treasures of darkness and riches hidden in secret places,
so that you may know that it is I, the Lord, the God of Israel,
who calls you by your name' (*Isaiah 45:3*).

NAOMI STARKEY

Magnificat

As a child, I loved dressing up. One of the items in our big dressing-up box was an old blue dressing gown, which came into its own each Christmas when my sister and I used to present a nativity play. Mary wore the dressing gown; blue is Mary's colour.

We are more used to hearing the story about Mary's visit to her cousin Elizabeth in Advent, as we prepare for Christmas, but there is a connection with May. On 31 May, some churches celebrate the visit of Mary to Elizabeth, and our readings this week note that special day, as well as Pentecost. In May, we see the signs of spring, a time of growth, so it is an appropriate season to consider the story of Mary and the baby growing within her.

Mary's song, which forms part of our reading this week, is often called the 'Magnificat'. The title comes from the first word of the poem in Latin. Benedict, the father of Western monasticism, set the Magnificat for use at one of the daily evening services. At the Reformation, it passed into the service of Evening Prayer in the Book of Common Prayer and, thus, it has been prayed by generations of Christians ever since.

Scholars think that the words of Mary's song draw on those of Hannah, when she responded in prayer and praise to God after being promised a son. If we look at 1 Samuel 2:1–10, we can see other similarities and, indeed, Hannah's words would have been used in worship by God's people, brought to mind at a time when God had done something else amazing. The implication is that Mary stands as one in a line of women of faith who were obedient to God.

The encounter between Mary and Elizabeth links together the stories of John and Jesus, too. Luke takes a long time getting to the story of the birth of Jesus, because he wants to set the scene well. As we read this passage, with hindsight, it gives us some clues about what the ministry of Jesus will be like.

Note: in order to mark the Visitation on Thursday, the reading for that day returns to the beginning of the story.

Rosie Ward

LUKE 1:39–42 (NRSV)

Filled with the Holy Spirit

In those days Mary set out and went with haste to a Judean town in the hill country, where she entered the house of Zechariah and greeted Elizabeth. When Elizabeth heard Mary's greeting, the child leaped in her womb. And Elizabeth was filled with the Holy Spirit and exclaimed with a loud cry, 'Blessed are you among women, and blessed is the fruit of your womb.'

There they are, an unmarried teenager and the ageing wife of a priest, in joint admiration at God's divine plan. The one so long awaited is finally coming.

Sometimes Luke is very matter-of-fact. Mary had met an angel. She had said 'Yes' to God and then the angel had gone, leaving Mary alone. As the implications began to sink in, it is hardly surprising that she should want to talk to someone. Why Elizabeth? We are given the clue a few verses earlier (v. 36). The angel tells Mary that her cousin has also conceived a son. So, if there is one person in the whole world to whom she can talk about her feelings, it is Elizabeth.

Elizabeth was beyond normal childbearing years and had been unable to have children. If she was going to have a child, it could only be the work of God. She is now six months pregnant—her condition is beyond doubt. Going to visit her is a way of proving that it is not all just a dream.

God's actions in speaking directly to Mary and Elizabeth show that women can hear and understand God's word as clearly and directly as men. Zechariah, Elizabeth's husband and a priest, the one who should have been in tune with God, had refused to believe the news (v. 18).

On this day of Pentecost, we remember that the Spirit was poured out on all people—men and women, slave and free. Are we fully receptive to God or do we sometimes think that he speaks only to others? Let us thank God for giving his Spirit to us and rejoice that, as he had special tasks for Elizabeth and Mary, so he has special tasks for us.

Prayer

Heavenly Father, thank you for sending your Spirit. Help me to be open to his empowering presence in my life.

ROSIE WARD

LUKE 1:42–45 (NRSV)

The greeting

[Elizabeth] exclaimed with a loud cry, 'Blessed are you among women, and blessed is the fruit of your womb. And why has this happened to me, that the mother of my Lord comes to me? For as soon as I heard the sound of your greeting, the child in my womb leaped for joy. And blessed is she who believed that there would be a fulfilment of what was spoken to her by the Lord.'

Filled with the Spirit, Elizabeth realises why Mary has come. She can recognise God in another because she is so close to God herself. The child whom she is carrying is part of God's plan, too—with the important role of preparing the way for his cousin.

So, Elizabeth is the first person to acknowledge that Mary is carrying the one who will be 'Lord'. The people of God knew that one day God would send a rescuer, but the promise had been made a long time ago and the worship of God was not all it might have been at that time, despite the best efforts of the prophets. Of all the people on earth then, Mary and Elizabeth alone knew that the Messiah was being formed in Mary's womb.

Elizabeth functions as a prophet, praising Mary for her belief and her joyous burst of praise must have fortified Mary. She singles out Mary's faith in believing what has been spoken, in contrast to Zechariah, who disbelieved the words of the angel. Mary has seen that Elizabeth is going to have a child; perhaps that confirmation took away any last doubts she might have had that all the angel said was true.

There are times when we find it hard to believe God or trust him. We are encouraged to give him our worries and anxieties, but sometimes a part of us worries that it cannot be that simple. God promises that he will never leave us or forsake us, but a part of us feels very alone. We read that God has good things in store for us, but we are impatient when life does not feel so good. This passage reminds us that what God has promised, he will fulfil.

Reflection

In what areas of my life am I finding it hard to trust God?

ROSIE WARD

LUKE 1:46–50 (NRSV)

The song

And Mary said, 'My soul magnifies the Lord, and my spirit rejoices in God my Saviour, for he has looked with favour on the lowliness of his servant. Surely, from now on all generations will call me blessed; for the Mighty One has done great things for me, and holy is his name. His mercy is for those who fear him from generation to generation.'

Mary's song begins with words of praise and thanksgiving to God, expressing her surprise that God has chosen her. She is filled with wonder at this because she knows that she is of low social and economic status. 'What, me?' is her response. God continues to surprise us and it is often to unsuspecting people that he comes and through whom he works, if only they will say yes.

Mary's words make huge claims: to say that 'from now on all generations will call me blessed' could sound like extraordinary arrogance, but it is all true and Mary affirms that it is as if the angel's words have already been fulfilled. God is the 'mighty one'—an Old Testament-style title—because he can do mighty things. He has 'mercy': in the past he has been faithful to his promises to his people and now, through Jesus, he will extend his mercy yet further.

As we have already seen, these words are very similar to those of Hannah, whose song begins, 'My heart exults in the Lord; my strength is exalted in my God' (1 Samuel 2:1). Mary's is the first song in Luke's Gospel, but is closely followed by that of a man, Zechariah, after the birth of his son John (Luke 1:68–79). Luke often pairs a story or incident involving a man with one about a woman—for example the man who lost a sheep and the woman who lost a coin (Luke 15)—to show that God cares equally for and works through both men and women. You may be able to think of other examples.

Mary's words here are a good pattern for us all: praising God for who he is and for what he has done.

Prayer

'My soul magnifies the Lord'—thank you, Lord, for all that you mean to me and all that you have done in my life.

ROSIE WARD

LUKE 1:51–55 (NRSV)

Revolution

'He has shown strength with his arm; he has scattered the proud in the thoughts of their hearts. He has brought down the powerful from their thrones, and lifted up the lowly; he has filled the hungry with good things, and sent the rich away empty. He has helped his servant Israel, in remembrance of his mercy, according to the promise he made to our ancestors, to Abraham and to his descendants for ever.'

William Temple, Archbishop of Canterbury in the early 1940s, warned his missionaries in India not to read the Magnificat in public, because the words were so inflammatory that they might start a revolution. The Magnificat has long been hailed as a song of liberation, a revolutionary text of conflict and victory.

The song speaks of bringing down the powerful from their thrones; this was actually happening at the time that I was writing these words, as people in various Middle Eastern and North African countries had risen up and overthrown their powerful rulers. Another former leader, who abused his authority and is said to have committed genocide, has recently been brought to trial. The proud have been scattered; the mighty have fallen. Ordinary people, who we hope will remain humble and not let power go to their heads, have been lifted up.

Reference to the 'arm' of God suggests his power—shown in such events as the exodus, his deliverance of his people Israel from the years of slavery in Egypt. 'His servant Israel' is a picture from Isaiah, where the prophet repeatedly speaks of the 'servant' who is to come. God kept his promise to Abraham, too, recalling a covenant right at the beginning of his relationship with his people. He has now acted to turn the usual values of the world upside down and usher in a new revolution.

The Church does not always look like a place where a revolution might happen, but God's revolution has begun. Our task is to work out in practice what has already been accomplished in principle.

Reflection

What does this mean for our world today? How am I called to work out God's revolution where I am?

ROSIE WARD

LUKE 1:39–41A (NRSV)

The visit

In those days Mary set out and went with haste to a Judean town in the hill country, where she entered the house of Zechariah and greeted Elizabeth. When Elizabeth heard Mary's greeting, the child leaped in her womb.

Luke is a book of journeys, and the first of these is that of Mary to Elizabeth, her cousin. Here two annunciations, to Zechariah and to Mary, come together as Luke unfolds the purpose of God. John will be the last prophet of the old covenant, bearing witness, even in the womb, to Christ, the promised Messiah.

Why did Mary go 'with haste'? We are not told of her immediate reaction to the angel's news after he had gone, but we can imagine it. She has been told that Elizabeth is also expecting a baby and knowing that her pregnancy is miraculous, too, gives her a sense of their having a shared destiny.

The reference to 'the hill country' is another link with the story of Hannah. Just as the story of Israel's royal house begins in the hill country (1 Samuel 1:1) with the story of Samuel's birth to Hannah, so the encounter between Mary and Elizabeth that introduces the story of Jesus begins in the hill country of Judea—the same area. Luke is shaping his story by referring back to another great story of God's people, which would be well known to his readers. As mentioned in the introduction to these readings, Mary stands in the line of women of faith who were obedient to the word of God, as Hannah was so many years before.

In this short passage, Luke ranges backwards into history and forwards into the future. I am constantly excited when I discover a connection that I have not seen before and am able to read one story in the light of the Bible's 'big story'. So many writers, speaking of God over so many generations, yet it is all one great story, of God's purposes for humankind.

Reflection

How well do I know the 'big story' of God's purposes? Is he challenging me to read more widely and dig more deeply so that I have a better understanding of the whole sweep of scripture?

ROSIE WARD

LUKE 1:51–55 (NRSV)

Filled with good things?

'He has shown strength with his arm; he has scattered the proud in the thoughts of their hearts. He has brought down the powerful from their thrones, and lifted up the lowly; he has filled the hungry with good things, and sent the rich away empty. He has helped his servant Israel, in remembrance of his mercy, according to the promise he made to our ancestors, to Abraham and to his descendants for ever.'

We return to Mary's remarkable song. As well as looking back and echoing the work of God in the past, it introduces key themes for the Gospel. The turning upside-down (or downside-up) of the world's values here is echoed in Jesus' manifesto in Luke 4, where he announces 'good news to the poor' (v. 18).

No wonder Mary's song is precious to all oppressed people for its vision of freedom from injustice. It looks ahead to the way Jesus lifted up women—the lowliest in his society—and challenged the proud. His teaching in the week before his death relates to the words here—for example, denouncing the Pharisees and lawyers for hypocrisy, suggesting that tax collectors and prostitutes might enter the kingdom of God and speaking up for the woman caught in adultery. These words of dramatic reversal also anticipate the resurrection, when the power of God triumphs over the powers that sent Jesus to his death. The words bring hope to the hopeless as they focus on God, who is true to his promises.

It is easy to read these familiar words and miss their practical implications. In our world, the lowly continue to be exploited and trampled underfoot by the powerful. There are all too many who are hungry and the numbers are only likely to increase with the effects of climate change and world pressures on food production. It is the poor who are sent empty away, while the rich (and we must include ourselves here) are filled with good things.

Prayer

Lord, thank you for the good things you have given me. Help me to share the riches that come from knowing Christ and to play my part in lifting up the lowly and filling the hungry.

ROSIE WARD

LUKE 1:56 (NRSV)

Shared destiny

And Mary remained with her about three months and then returned to her home.

This verse concludes the story of Mary's visit to Elizabeth. We are probably meant to assume that Mary left before the birth of John, since she plays no part in the story. Why did she leave at this time—*just* at the point when her relative might have valued the help and companionship of a close family member such as Mary?

Luke makes the effort to say how long Mary stayed. This could just be because, as his introduction to the Gospel suggests, he wants to give an 'orderly account' (1:1) of what happened. From time to time, people argue that the events surrounding the birth of Jesus are too impossible to believe, but it could be that the reference to the time here, as earlier in the angel's words about Elizabeth being in the sixth month of her pregnancy, is part of Luke's attempt to assure us that the events he is describing really happened.

Mary returns home before the birth of John the Baptist. She has yet to deal with the reaction of Joseph and, no doubt, many others to what appears to be a criminal breach of her betrothal to him. It is not always helpful to try to harmonise the different Gospel accounts, but the scene where Mary is discovered to be pregnant, which we read about only in Matthew's Gospel, seems to follow neatly on here.

Mary has seen what the necessary preparations for a birth are, she has shared her good news with her cousin and she has no doubt discussed the significance of the miraculous process in which they are both involved. How we would love to know more about those three months that Mary and Elizabeth spent together!

The story reminds us of the importance of friendship and companionship. We need people who can accompany us, those young in the faith looking to those who have travelled longer, and, when we share our stories of God's goodness and hear the stories of others, we share a double blessing.

Reflection

Who are the people who have encouraged you on your faith journey?
Who can you encourage today?

ROSIE WARD

Mark 1—8

Mark's is the shortest Gospel, often given to seekers or new believers. In the next three weeks, we will read about half of it—up to the 'hinge' of the Gospel in chapter 8, where Jesus asks the disciples what they think about his identity and begins to prophesy his death at the hands of the authorities. I will comment on the first four chapters and Stephen Rand on the second four.

The most frequently used word in Mark is 'immediately'. He tells of events at a breakneck speed, leaving out much of the detail we find in the other Gospels. His is, if you like, the tabloid Gospel, with striking 'headlines', simple language and fast-paced storytelling. It is not, however, written to sensationalise. Mark selects his stories purposefully, to answer the question the disciples pose in the last reading of my section: 'Who then is this?' Later, Jesus himself addresses this same question to the disciples: 'Who do people say that I am?... But who do you say that I am?' (Mark 8:27–29).

In the first half of the Gospel, Mark answers this implicitly, by showing the power of Jesus over not just sicknesses or spiritual oppression but the whole of creation. If the Gospel ended at 9:1, however, we could get a very distorted impression of that power. In chapters 9—16, Jesus demonstrates that his power is not for show or for personal advantage, but is exercised with meekness and vulnerability; that the kingdom he announces is an 'upside-down kingdom', where children are at the centre, the first is last and the last first and death leads to life.

So chapters 1—8 prepare for the shocking prophecy of 8:31 by showing how Jesus' brand of self-sacrificing power provokes opposition from the religious authorities. They are too busy defending their own patch to recognise God at work in anyone else. Mark 1—8 teaches us to be ready for new wisdom and new acts of God. When we say that 'Jesus Christ is the same yesterday and today and for ever' (Hebrews 13:8), we should not mean that Jesus is never surprising. Indeed, Mark shows us that Jesus is always surprising.

Veronica Zundel

Mark 1:1–8 (NRSV, abridged)

Good news or bad?

The beginning of the good news of Jesus Christ, the Son of God. As it is written in the prophet Isaiah, 'See, I am sending my messenger ahead of you, who will prepare your way...' John the baptiser appeared in the wilderness, proclaiming a baptism of repentance for the forgiveness of sins. And people from the whole Judean countryside and all the people of Jerusalem were going out to him, and were baptised by him in the river Jordan, confessing their sins... He proclaimed, 'The one who is more powerful than I is coming after me... I have baptised you with water; but he will baptise you with the Holy Spirit.'

When we try to proclaim 'the good news', why do we sometimes feel that we have to start with the bad news? We try to persuade people they are sinners bound for hell, just so we can tell them Jesus will save them from this fate. I do not get the impression that is what John the Baptist did. He simply declared the opportunity for forgiveness—he seemed to think people would already know they needed it. Certainly, whatever he did say, he attracted crowds. Forgiveness under Jewish Law was a complicated matter of animal sacrifices and priestly actions; baptism, with its powerful symbolism of being totally washed clean, was a much simpler way.

'The beginning of the good news' (v. 1) is still repentance, but this does not have to mean believing you are the worst of sinners. The Greek word used simply means 'a change of mind' and many people acknowledge that they need a new start. I know of a single mother with four children, two with special needs; she is ill herself and vulnerably housed. I would love her to recognise and follow Jesus and know the care and provision that God gives. It would take a change of mind on her part, but not necessarily for her to believe she is full of sin. I just long for her to discover that the one who came after has untold riches of spirit to give her.

Reflection

'Prepare the way of the Lord, make his paths straight' (v. 3).
How might you help prepare a friend for meeting Jesus?

Veronica Zundel

MARK 1:9–13 (NRSV)

Beasts and angels

In those days Jesus came from Nazareth of Galilee and was baptised by John in the Jordan. And just as he was coming up out of the water, he saw the heavens torn apart and the Spirit descending like a dove on him. And a voice came from heaven, 'You are my Son, the Beloved; with you I am well pleased.' And the Spirit immediately drove him out into the wilderness. He was in the wilderness forty days, tempted by Satan; and he was with the wild beasts; and the angels waited on him.

How many people long for their father or mother to say just once that they love and are pleased by them? Jesus' affirmation from his Father God must have been a moment of great joy—the heavenly voice was not just for the sake of the onlookers. It also affirmed his decision to undergo baptism, identifying with sinful humanity.

If you heard a voice from God, would you expect some great blessing to follow? I am sure you would, but 'the Spirit immediately drove him out into the wilderness' (v. 12). Elijah had a similar experience after his victory over the prophets of Baal: 'He… went a day's journey into the wilderness, and came and sat down under a solitary broom tree. He asked that he might die: 'It is enough; now, O Lord, take away my life, for I am no better than my ancestors' (1 Kings 19:4).

It seems to be some sort of natural or spiritual law that, after a spiritual high, we may experience a time of severe testing. Paradoxically, this may be a sign of how much God loves us and wants to shape us in Christ's image: 'for the Lord disciplines those whom he loves, and chastises every child whom he accepts' (Hebrews 12:6).

Jesus 'was with the wild beasts'. Artist Stanley Spencer painted a wonderful series of pictures of Jesus in the wilderness with various animals—foxes and cubs, hens and chicks. I love best the one of Jesus holding a scorpion in his hand: his expression seems to convey how much he loves his creation and sorrows for the pain and hostility in it.

Prayer

Lord, when wild beasts surround me, send your angels.

VERONICA ZUNDEL

MARK 1:21–27 (NRSV, ABRIDGED)

Authority

They went to Capernaum; and when the sabbath came, [Jesus] entered the synagogue and taught... Just then there was in their synagogue a man with an unclean spirit, and he cried out, 'What have you to do with us, Jesus of Nazareth? Have you come to destroy us? I know who you are, the Holy One of God.' But Jesus rebuked him, saying, 'Be silent, and come out of him!' And the unclean spirit, throwing him into convulsions and crying with a loud voice, came out of him. They were all amazed, and they kept on asking one another, 'What is this? A new teaching—with authority! He commands even the unclean spirits, and they obey him.'

Casting out evil spirits has a bad name today, with some churches even trying to 'exorcise' misbehaving young children or the mentally ill. Yet every Anglican diocese has a diocesan exorcist, and I believe that there is a spiritual force of evil in the world, greater than the sum of human sin. The vital message about this force, though, is that Jesus has already defeated it—it just won't lie down yet.

This is the first miracle Mark records and it is significant because it shows that Jesus has power over all that damages and limits human life. It is also significant that it takes place on the sabbath, though he gets away with it this time. Notice that the passage starts with 'they': Jesus has already started to call the twelve disciples—at this stage just fishermen Peter and Andrew, James and John. Perhaps their company gave him the courage to perform this healing (he was human, after all, and it was not easy to confront the religious authorities, let alone a demon). Perhaps he is beginning to show them what it means to 'fish for people' (v. 17).

'A new teaching—with authority!' For some, authority is a matter of shouting louder and not admitting any uncertainty. I think Jesus' authority was more an inner conviction about who he was—'the Beloved'—and what God had called him to do.

Reflection

'The Son of God was revealed for this purpose,
to destroy the works of the devil' (1 John 3:8).

VERONICA ZUNDEL

MARK 2:3–12 (NRSV, ABRIDGED)

Sin and sorrow

Then some people came, bringing to [Jesus] a paralysed man... And when they could not bring him to Jesus because of the crowd, they removed the roof... When Jesus saw their faith, he said to the paralytic, 'Son, your sins are forgiven.' Now some of the scribes were sitting there, questioning in their hearts, 'Why does this fellow speak in this way? It is blasphemy!...' [Jesus] said to them, '... Which is easier, to say to the paralytic, "Your sins are forgiven", or to say, "Stand up and take your mat and walk"? But so that you may know that the Son of Man has authority on earth to forgive sins... I say to you, stand up, take your mat and go to your home.' And he stood up, and immediately took the mat and went out before all of them; so that they were all amazed and glorified God.

The man was not paralysed because of his sins. Jesus made that quite clear in John 9:1–3. In fact, if he had friends willing to carry him to Jesus and lower him through the roof, he must have been a man who inspired great loyalty. Every miracle in Mark, though, is a hint as to Jesus' nature and a confrontation with those who opposed him. Here he goes right to the heart of the matter: we all need forgiveness and reconciliation with God.

'Who can forgive sins but God alone?' (v. 7) object the religious experts. Jesus, in a typically Jewish way, answers by wordlessly posing another question, 'Who can heal the lame but God alone?' In this way, he demonstrates that he is sent by God and does God's work.

So what about those who are not healed, like my friend Lesley, who died of cancer recently? Does that mean their sins are not forgiven? Lesley's faith and radiance as she went through the process of dying gives the lie to that. We cannot know why God heals some (and I know God does: I have met healed people) and not others, but forgiveness is ready for anyone who turns to Jesus for help.

Reflection

This is Jesus' first use of the title 'Son of Man'.
What does this title mean to you?

VERONICA ZUNDEL

MARK 2:13–17 (NRSV, ABRIDGED)

Calling in the outsiders

Jesus went out again beside the sea; the whole crowd gathered around him, and he taught them. As he was walking along, he saw Levi son of Alphaeus sitting at the tax booth, and he said to him, 'Follow me.' And he got up and followed him. And as he sat at dinner in Levi's house, many tax collectors and sinners were also sitting with Jesus and his disciples… When the scribes of the Pharisees saw that he was eating with sinners and tax collectors, they said to his disciples, 'Why does he eat with tax collectors and sinners?' When Jesus heard this, he said to them, 'Those who are well have no need of a physician, but those who are sick; I have come to call not the righteous but sinners.'

To eat with someone is to share fellowship with them, to make yourself vulnerable to them and open to the friendship they have to give you. Some members of exclusive sects refuse to eat with people, even members of their family, who do not belong to their sect.

Jesus has no time for such exclusivity. If you wonder why tax collectors were scorned, there are two reasons: they worked for the hated Roman occupiers and they collected more than was due so they could cream off the profit. We could compare them to the loan sharks of today who infest poor areas. Jesus, though, attracted such people—people such as Levi, whom we usually know as Matthew. What was it about him that called them to him? Perhaps a clue is in this little statement from John 8:15: 'I judge no one.' Likewise, Jesus urges us to follow his example: 'Do not judge, so that you may not be judged' (Matthew 7:1) or, as I like to put it, 'Being a Christian does not mainly consist of disapproving of people.'

'Sinners' in Jesus' context were often just poor people who could not afford the correct animal sacrifice or had to break the sabbath to survive economically. Today, we might think of them as 'the underclass'. How good are we at being church for such people?

Reflection

Notice that Jesus' call to Levi is not 'Believe in me', but 'Follow me.'

VERONICA ZUNDEL

MARK 3:1–2, 4–6 (NRSV)

Good is always good

Again [Jesus] entered the synagogue, and a man was there who had a withered hand. They watched him to see whether he would cure him on the sabbath, so that they might accuse him… Then he said to them, 'Is it lawful to do good or to do harm on the sabbath, to save life or to kill?' But they were silent. He looked around at them with anger; he was grieved at their hardness of heart and said to the man, 'Stretch out your hand.' He stretched it out, and his hand was restored. The Pharisees went out and immediately conspired with the Herodians against him, how to destroy him.

My church had a long debate about whether or not two individuals were eligible for membership. It ended up unresolved, because the church could not agree. It has saddened me, because I felt that part of the church was putting principle before people and I believe Jesus' attitude to the sabbath here teaches us that we should always put people before principle.

Jesus has already got into trouble for the fact that his disciples plucked ears of grain to eat as they walked through the fields on the sabbath (2:23–28). His pronouncement then was that 'rhe sabbath was made for humankind, not humankind for the sabbath' (v. 27). In other words, people come before principles. Now many eyes are watching to see if he will continue to 'transgress' against their religious laws.

Yet again, in this incident, Jesus answers their questioning eyes with another question. At root, he is asking, 'What do you call good?' Their idea of goodness was keeping all the rules and the sabbath rules were central to their lives. Jesus prompts them to look at what is really good: to save life and heal the hurting. Such actions cannot be bad, even on the sabbath. We will see in tomorrow's reading how they fail to recognise this and so cannot receive God's forgiveness—because they do not acknowledge their need for it.

Reflection

'He has told you, O mortal, what is good; and what does the Lord require of you but to do justice, and to love kindness, and to walk humbly with your God?' (Micah 6:8).

VERONICA ZUNDEL

MARK 3:19–29 (NRSV, ABRIDGED)

Only good conquers evil

Then [Jesus] went home; and the crowd came together again, so that they could not even eat... And the scribes who came down from Jerusalem said, 'He has Beelzebul, and by the ruler of the demons he casts out demons.' And he... spoke to them in parables, 'How can Satan cast out Satan? If a kingdom is divided against itself, that kingdom cannot stand... no one can enter a strong man's house and plunder his property without first tying up the strong man; then indeed the house can be plundered. Truly I tell you, people will be forgiven for their sins and whatever blasphemies they utter; but whoever blasphemes against the Holy Spirit can never have forgiveness, but is guilty of an eternal sin.'

Binding the Strong Man is a 'political reading' of the Gospel of Mark by theologian and activist Ched Myers. In it, he suggests that Jesus' mission was not just 'spiritual' salvation, but confronting and challenging the powers that kept the poor and vulnerable oppressed. If this is true, 'Satan' means not just the demons he cast out of individuals but also the political and religious powers that oppressed and exploited people.

This is not to say that Jesus engaged in politics in the sense of starting a party or running for office, but, rather, the spiritual challenges he issued had a strong political dimension. You cannot take the Bible out of politics or politics out of the Bible: if you do, you end up with a politics with un-Christian values and a Bible that is so heavenly minded it is of no earthly good.

What, then, is the 'sin [or 'blasphemy'] against the Holy Spirit'? Many people from a Christian background have lain awake at night fearing they have committed it, but the context here clearly shows that it is not a sin you can commit accidentally, for it is simply calling something bad which God has called good. Among other things, this means that when we see non-Christians doing good things, we are to rejoice in this as God's work, not condemn them because they are not Christian.

Prayer

Lord Jesus, help me to discern what is truly good, and what is truly evil.

VERONICA ZUNDEL

MARK 4:2–9 (NRSV, ABRIDGED)

Seeds we sow

[Jesus] began to teach them many things in parables, and in his teaching he said to them: 'Listen! A sower went out to sow. And as he sowed, some seed fell on the path, and the birds came and ate it up. Other seed fell on rocky ground, where it did not have much soil... And when the sun rose, it was scorched; and since it had no root, it withered away. Other seed fell among thorns, and the thorns grew up and choked it, and it yielded no grain. Other seed fell into good soil and brought forth grain, growing up and increasing and yielding thirty and sixty and a hundredfold.' And he said, 'Let anyone with ears to hear listen!'

We may know this story so well that we read it almost without thinking. Maybe the first thing to note is that Jesus was a carpenter, not a farmer, yet he appears to know plenty about how seeds are sown and what happens to them. He must have chosen this metaphor because many of his audience would have grown crops that succeeded or failed.

This is encouraging to those of us who try to communicate the good news. It suggests that we can frame the gospel in language that makes sense to our audience, even if it is not our normal language. We can find common ground and talk about experiences in modern life: the gospel in terms of Facebook, perhaps, or in terms of what it is like to live in a city. This requires inventiveness and insight, but Jesus promised that 'what you are to say will be given to you at that time; for it is not you who speak, but the Spirit of your Father speaking through you' (Matthew 10:19–20).

Another aspect to notice is that Jesus here acknowledges that life—even life with him—will contain some failure as well as some success. Not every day will be a good one; not every job we do will be our ideal job; and not everyone we baptise will become a growing disciple—but we have to go on 'sowing'.

Reflection

How might you retell this parable for a modern, non-rural audience?

VERONICA ZUNDEL

MARK 4:13–20 (NRSV, ABRIDGED)

Grounds for complaint?

[Jesus said] 'The sower sows the word. These are the ones on the path... When they hear, Satan immediately comes and takes away the word that is sown in them. And these are the ones sown on rocky ground... they have no root, and endure only for a while; then, when trouble or persecution arises on account of the word, immediately they fall away. And others are those sown among the thorns: these are the ones who hear the word, but the cares of the world, and the lure of wealth, and the desire for other things come in and choke the word, and it yields nothing. And these are the ones sown on the good soil: they hear the word and accept it and bear fruit.'

Which ground do you identify with? I sometimes fear I'm the third kind, where the growing seed is choked by worries and greed. Is this parable meant to challenge people as to which kind of ground they are, though, or is it addressed to sowers, to explain the varying results that will come of their sowing? It may be both. Jesus tells the parable to 'a very large crowd', who may be thought of as ground, but then he explains it to the disciples alone, who may be thought of as sowers.

If we are those who receive the word—Sunday by Sunday in sermons or in our private Bible study—we can ask ourselves how we can become more 'fertile'. I have suffered physical infertility and know there are things you can do to increase your chances of conceiving a baby. Perhaps there are things we can do to increase our chances of bearing the fruit of the Spirit—opening our hearts, growing spiritual roots, clearing away the weeds.

If we are those—as I am—who deliver the word to others, we can think about where to sow, how to identify the fertile ground. Today we remember Barnabas, the 'son of encouragement': because he recognised Paul's 'fertile ground', many others have heard God's word.

Reflection

'Those who abide in me and I in them bear much fruit, because apart from me you can do nothing' (John 15:5).

VERONICA ZUNDEL

MARK 4:35–41 (NRSV, ABRIDGED)

Asleep on duty

When evening had come, [Jesus] said to them, 'Let us go across to the other side.' And leaving the crowd behind, they took him with them in the boat... A great windstorm arose, and the waves beat into the boat, so that the boat was already being swamped. But he was in the stern, asleep on the cushion; and they woke him up and said to him, 'Teacher, do you not care that we are perishing?' He woke up and rebuked the wind, and said to the sea, 'Peace! Be still!' Then the wind ceased, and there was a dead calm. He said to them, 'Why are you afraid? Have you still no faith?' And they were filled with great awe and said to one another, 'Who then is this, that even the wind and the sea obey him?'

We do not know whether Jesus chose to cross the lake to teach and heal other groups of people or if he was looking for some quiet space with his disciples. He was clearly tired, as the rocking waves lulled him to sleep (I have slept on a boat and the movement is very soporific.) I expect the disciples were happy for him to get some rest while the waves were calm. When things got rough, however, they turned to him. Did they perhaps dimly guess that he could do something about the storm or did they just want him awake with them as they drowned?

Jesus does not 'cry or lift up his voice' (Isaiah 42:2), but gently, calmly speaks peace to the sea. We have seen his power over demons, sin and sickness, and now we see his power over creation. It is not blustering, dominating power, but a quiet, confident power that comes from trust in God.

Just as I was writing this, a violent hailstorm erupted outside. When our life feels full of storms, Jesus may appear to be sleeping on the job. But he is still with us and if we cry out to him, he will respond. Can we, too, speak peace into conflict and fear?

Prayer

'Hear, O Lord, when I cry aloud, be gracious to me and answer me!' (Psalm 27:7).

VERONICA ZUNDEL

MARK 5:2, 7–15 (TNIV, ABRIDGED)

Good news: in his right mind

> A man with an evil spirit came from the tombs to meet [Jesus]... He shouted at the top of his voice, 'What do you want with me, Jesus, Son of the Most High God?'... Then Jesus asked him, 'What is your name?' 'My name is Legion,' he replied, 'for we are many.'... The demons begged Jesus, 'Send us among the pigs; allow us to go into them.'... The people went out to see what had happened. When they came to Jesus, they saw the man... sitting there, dressed and in his right mind.

Jesus has crossed the lake 'to the country of the Gerasenes' (v. 1), outside Jewish territory, in a Gentile area. The good news is not to be confined: it must break out to the whole world (13:10).

This tormented individual was probably a Gentile; living among the tombs definitely made him unclean. Mark is emphasising that no one is cut off from God's transforming power in Jesus. That's good news. Evil forces almost beyond counting had taken control of the man's existence, but the starting point for Jesus is to ask his name. Jesus refused to define him by his mental state, his ethnic identity or his religious status: he was an individual, made in God's image—and he had a name.

Meeting Jesus changed his life: he ended up 'in his right mind'. Yes, the destruction of the pigs as part of his cure (5:13) is a difficult part of the story. Perhaps it demonstrates, above all, the relative value of one human life.

I have a friend who visited a town in Africa where a man lived by the main crossroads. He would strip off his clothes and harangue passers-by, who gave him a wide berth. My friend returned several months later. There was no sign of the man at the crossroads. He enquired what had happened. A Christian in the town had stopped avoiding him and invited him into his home. This display of care and compassion had transformed the man's life. He was now dressed and in his right mind. Jesus is still good news.

Reflect

Whom do we avoid when we could introduce them to Jesus?

STEPHEN RAND

MARK 5:22–23, 35–36, 40–42 (TNIV, ABRIDGED)

Good news: life!

One of the synagogue leaders, named Jairus, came, and when he saw Jesus, he... pleaded earnestly with him, 'My little daughter is dying. Please come and put your hands on her so that she will be healed and live.'... Some people came from the house... 'Your daughter is dead,' they said... Jesus told him, 'Don't be afraid; just believe.'... [He] went in where the child was. He took her by the hand and said to her, 'Talitha koum!' (which means 'Little girl, I say to you, get up!'). Immediately the girl stood up and began to walk around (she was twelve years old).

Mark continues to emphasise the inclusive and transforming ministry of Jesus. He is now back on home territory and the expressed need comes from a leader of the local synagogue, but the one who needs Jesus is both young and a girl. Her place in the culture and the community would not have been high. She would have been excluded from full participation in the religious life of her day—but not from the mercy of God. Jesus was even prepared to break the rules and touch her dead body, insistent that people come before religious rituals and tradition.

Jairus had faith. If only he could get Jesus to his little girl in time... but he fails. She has died. At his moment of despair, Jesus encourages him—'don't be afraid'—and then urges him, using the continuous tense: 'keep believing.'

Moments of personal crisis often drive people either closer to God or further away from him. My wife Susan and I had a friend whose mother was diagnosed with cancer. The mother found a strength of faith that enabled her to witness to God's presence in the remaining few weeks of her life; our friend gave up on a God who could allow such suffering and loss. God does not guarantee his followers an escape from every crisis, but he does promise his presence.

Reflection

Today, do you need to hear the reassuring words of Jesus, 'Keep on believing'? Faith can cast out fear because Jesus can be trusted. Jairus' daughter came back to life; the gospel promises those who believe an even greater resurrection—to eternal life.

STEPHEN RAND

Mark 5:24–34 (TNIV, abridged)

Good news: clean again

A large crowd pressed around [Jesus]. And a woman was there who had been subject to bleeding for twelve years... When she heard about Jesus, she came up behind him in the crowd and touched his cloak, because she thought, 'If I just touch his clothes, I will be healed.' Immediately her bleeding stopped... At once Jesus realised that power had gone out from him. He turned around in the crowd and asked, 'Who touched my clothes?'... Then the woman, knowing what had happened to her, came and fell at his feet and, trembling with fear, told him the whole truth. He said to her, 'Daughter, your faith has healed you. Go in peace.'

Jairus is desperate to get Jesus to his dying daughter. The crowd is slowing down—and there is a woman whose need is just as desperate. She has suffered twelve years of misery, embarrassment and debilitating ill health which makes her unclean—cut off from human touch and participation in worship. She knew Jesus was her only hope. She was convinced that if only she could touch him, all would be different.

This last element is the strange part of the story. The belief that touching a holy person will heal sickness has been common in many cultures, but she must have known that, in her culture, to do so would transfer her uncleanness to him. Perhaps that is why she focused on touching no more than his clothes. Perhaps she was convinced that Jesus was too holy to be tainted by her touch. Jesus stops, almost cruelly, to expose the woman; he is determined to ensure that faith, not a magic touch, is seen to be at the heart of the miracle.

Something deeper is also revealed. Earlier, Jesus had stated, 'The sabbath was made for people, not people for the sabbath; so the Son of Man is lord even of the sabbath' (2:27–28). Again, Mark demonstrates that Jesus is above ritual and tradition. He was prepared to accept uncleanness so that she could be clean again. Healing, renewal, a fresh start, peace... that's good news.

Reflection

Whenever we are desperate for Jesus, he will never turn away; he always has time for us.

Stephen Rand

MARK 6:31–34 (TNIV)

Good news: compassion

Then, because so many people were coming and going that they did not even have a chance to eat, [Jesus] said to them, 'Come with me by yourselves to a quiet place and get some rest.' So they went away by themselves in a boat to a solitary place. But many who saw them leaving recognised them and ran on foot from all the towns and got there ahead of them. When Jesus landed and saw a large crowd, he had compassion on them, because they were like sheep without a shepherd.

You may know what it is like to be hounded by people, to be in demand at every waking moment. Mothers of small children know it. In my experience with Tearfund, there were many seeking to meet the desperate needs of the poor and destitute who knew it. The experience can be destructive, producing emotional and spiritual frailty as physical tiredness takes its toll.

In this situation, Jesus demonstrates his compassion. The large crowd may be like sheep, but it is made up of people created in the image of God, each an individual in need of his love. Jesus reveals the good news that 'because of the Lord's great love we are not consumed, for his compassions never fail. They are new every morning; great is your faithfulness' (Lamentations 3:22–23). Praise God that this is a reality we can experience day by day.

Mark chooses his words carefully. Jesus is the answer to a prayer first uttered hundreds of years earlier by Moses and first fulfilled in his Hebrew namesake, Joshua: 'May the Lord, the God of every human spirit, appoint someone over this community to go out and come in before them, one who will lead them out and bring them in, so the Lord's people will not be like sheep without a shepherd' (Numbers 27:16–17).

The compassion of Jesus reveals the truth of God's nature.

Prayer

Lord, when I am at the end of my tether, desperate for rest, in your mercy grant me enough resource that I may be a channel of your peace. Help me to see past the crowd and recognise individuals in need of your compassion.

STEPHEN RAND

MARK 6:35–42 (TNIV, ABRIDGED)

Good news: meeting need

It was late in the day, so his disciples came to him [and said]... 'Send the people away so that they can... buy themselves something to eat.' But he answered, 'You give them something to eat.' They said to him, 'That would take almost a year's wages!...' 'How many loaves do you have?' he asked. 'Go and see.' When they found out, they said, 'Five—and two fish.' Then Jesus directed them to have all the people sit down... in groups of hundreds and fifties. Taking the five loaves and the two fish... he gave them to his disciples to set before the people... They all ate and were satisfied.

The echo of Moses we noted yesterday continues here: a great crowd in the desert, taught and miraculously fed. Even the organisational details have the same echo—Moses grouped the people in 'thousands, hundreds, fifties and tens' (Exodus 18:21) when he delegated leadership and Jesus tells his disciples to organise the crowd in a similar way.

Jesus very clearly gives responsibility to his disciples to take the lead in meeting this need. They want to send the people away, but Jesus wants them to be agents for his divine activity. They can see the size of the challenge, but Jesus focuses on the resources to be shared. The miracle is that they do what they are told.

Many churches have someone who is ready instantly to explain why something cannot be done. John's Gospel reveals Philip as the mathematical genius who could look at the crowd, assess its size, multiply it by the average wage and divide it by the price of bread—yes, a man who knew the price of bread!

It is a great gospel truth that God has a purpose for me and for you: he wants to use you to change the world. When we come to him empty-handed, he will give us his resources to share with others. Every blessing we receive is a blessing to be shared.

Prayer

Lord, help me not to be deterred by the size of a challenge, but to trust in you for the necessary resources. Thank you for using people like me as your agents of change.

STEPHEN RAND

MARK 6:47–51A (TNIV)

Good news: the presence of God's Son

When evening came, the boat was in the middle of the lake, and [Jesus] was alone on land. He saw the disciples straining at the oars, because the wind was against them. Shortly before dawn he went out to them, walking on the lake. He was about to pass by them, but when they saw him walking on the lake, they thought he was a ghost. They cried out, because they all saw him and were terrified. Immediately he spoke to them and said, 'Take courage! It is I. Don't be afraid.' Then he climbed into the boat with them, and the wind died down.

I wonder how popular Mark was with the disciples? He tells this story, and then adds, 'They were completely amazed, for they had not understood about the loaves; their hearts were hardened' (v. 51–52). What had they not understood?

Mark has been taking the reader on a journey, using his language carefully. He has alluded to Jesus in terms of Moses and also David, the shepherd-king. In this story, he presses further, pursuing the theme of his Gospel from the start: Jesus is more than a prophet and a king; he is the divine Son of God.

There are three very specific indications in this story. First, he walks on the water. In Job's magnificent description of the Creator God, he says, 'He alone… treads on the waves of the sea' (Job 9:8). Second, the words he uses to reveal himself when they are terrified, translated here as 'It is I', are an echo of words used by God himself: 'I, even I, am he who comforts you' (Isaiah 51:12). Third, of course, he demonstrates the power of the Creator over creation, as the storm is stilled.

The application is obvious. Perhaps today is the very day that you need to hear the voice of Jesus saying, 'Take courage! It is I. Don't be afraid.' Perhaps you can identify with the disciples, straining and struggling against the wind, in the dark, all at sea. Jesus did not come quickly, but he did come—and he brought peace.

Prayer

Son of God, show your divine power in calming my storm
and grant me the peace of your presence.

STEPHEN RAND

MARK 7:5–9 (TNIV, ABRIDGED)

Good news: freedom from tradition

The Pharisees and teachers of the law asked Jesus, 'Why don't your disciples live according to the tradition of the elders instead of eating their food with defiled hands?' He replied, 'Isaiah was right when he prophesied about you hypocrites; as it is written: "These people honour me with their lips, but their hearts are far from me. They worship me in vain; their teachings are merely human rules." ... You have a fine way of setting aside the commands of God in order to observe your own traditions!'

The prophets had a recurring theme: God loathes hypocrisy. In particular, he hates the hypocrisy of worship that is only on the lips and not in lives. 'I cannot bear your evil assemblies... When you spread out your hands in prayer, I will hide my eyes from you... Stop doing wrong, learn to do right! Seek justice, encourage the oppressed' (from Isaiah 1).

The prophets are echoed by Jesus: he hates elaborate constructions of rules and regulations which overlook the fact that people, not procedures, are what matter most. 'Woe to you... you hypocrites! You give a tenth of your spices—mint, dill and cumin. But you have neglected the more important matters of the law—justice, mercy and faithfulness' (Matthew 23:23).

The apostles repeat the challenge to the early Church. God's people will always tend to substitute freedom with formality, transformation with tradition. How quickly new churches can create new traditions!

You may already be thinking of the examples in your church. Do people worry more about what the person at the front wears than what they say and how they live? Is the style of music more important than the hearts of the worshippers? Tradition in itself is not the problem. The biblical principle is clear: lives lived for others matter far more than religious observance: 'Religion that God our Father accepts as pure and faultless is this: to look after orphans and widows in their distress and to keep oneself from being polluted by the world' (James 1:27).

Prayer

Dear Lord, let my whole life worship you in Spirit and in truth. May your Church model a gospel of grace and freedom, not rules and regulations.

STEPHEN RAND

MARK 7:25–30 (TNIV)

Good news for outsiders

A woman whose little daughter was possessed by an evil spirit came and fell at his feet. The woman was a Greek, born in Syrian Phoenicia. She begged Jesus to drive the demon out of her daughter. 'First let the children eat all they want,' he told her, 'for it is not right to take the children's bread and toss it to the dogs.' 'Lord,' she replied, 'even the dogs under the table eat the children's crumbs.' Then he told her, 'For such a reply, you may go; the demon has left your daughter.' She went home and found her child lying on the bed, and the demon gone.

Jesus has rejected the religious traditions of his day. Mark brings this to life with an example of Jesus reaching out to someone apparently outside the scope of God's grace. His gospel is concerned with the same reality of bringing God to those who do not know him that was entrusted to the people of Israel in the first place.

Everything seemed to be stacked against this desperate mother. She was a woman and a Gentile; Jesus should have had nothing to do with her. All the same, her daughter is healed; she knows God's blessings through her encounter with his Son.

It is not just that God is pleased when 'outsiders' receive the good news; that is the whole point of the good news. Part of what makes the gospel good news is that no one is excluded. Even now, in my work with Open Doors, I hear of people who have taken the gospel to those who have persecuted them, bringing reconciliation rather than retaliation.

In our churches, we face a different pressure. It is so much easier when I worship with 'people like me', but, if we are not sensitised to those outside our circle, we will be dishonouring the one we worship. For us, 'outsiders' may be defined by their ethnicity, social class, or sexuality. It is not enough just to be welcoming to those who come to us—the final words of Jesus were 'Go into all the world…' (Mark 16:15).

Reflection

Jesus went out of his way and out of his religious and cultural comfort zone to reach 'outsiders'.

STEPHEN RAND

MARK 8:22–25 (TNIV, ABRIDGED)

Good news: seeing clearly

They came to Bethsaida, and some people brought a blind man and begged Jesus to touch him... When he had spit on the man's eyes and put his hands on him, Jesus asked, 'Do you see anything?' He looked up and said, 'I see people; they look like trees walking around.' Once more Jesus put his hands on the man's eyes. Then his eyes were opened, his sight was restored, and he saw everything clearly.

'Your God will come... he will come to save you. Then will the eyes of the blind be opened...' This is part of Isaiah 35 (vv. 4–5)—a magnificent hymn of prophetic praise about the impact of the coming of God's salvation. So the healing of a blind man is a sure sign that the kingdom of God is indeed at hand.

This story follows immediately after an exchange between Jesus and his disciples in which Jesus says, 'Do you still not see or understand? Are your hearts hardened? Do you have eyes but fail to see...?' (Mark 8:17–18). Mark identifies this miracle as having something to say about the disciples' own situation—they were in need of a further opening of their spiritual eyes in order to be able to understand the gospel fully.

One of my worst fears is that I will be sure I understand my faith fully but, in fact, will be at the stage of seeing people like trees. I want and I need Jesus to keep touching my eyes. Only when I see clearly can I act effectively. Clarity of vision—literally and metaphorically—is vital to walking by faith and following God's purposes.

More than 30 years ago, I travelled round the UK with Vijayan Pavamani, a Tearfund partner from India. Night after night, he preached about the need for us all to have a 'second touch' from Jesus. His eyes had been opened to see the needs of the street children and drug addicts of Kolkata. And, because his eyes had been opened, many had come to know Jesus for themselves.

Reflection

Lord Jesus, grant me clear spiritual vision so that I may see you and all you have made—people and planet—in the light of your glory and grace.

STEPHEN RAND

MARK 8:27–33 (TNIV, ABRIDGED)

Good news: the cross (1)

Jesus asked [his disciples], 'Who do people say I am?' They replied, 'Some say John the Baptist; others say Elijah; and still others, one of the prophets.' 'But what about you?' he asked. 'Who do you say I am?' Peter answered, 'You are the Messiah.'... He then began to teach them that the Son of Man must suffer many things and be rejected by the elders, the chief priests and the teachers of the law, and that he must be killed and after three days rise again. He spoke plainly about this, and Peter took him aside and began to rebuke him... [Jesus] rebuked Peter. 'Get behind me, Satan!' he said.

Here is further evidence of the spiritual blindness we reflected on yesterday. No sooner has Peter recognised that Jesus is the promised Messiah than he misunderstands what it will mean. This prompts Jesus to deliver a crushing rebuke: 'You do not have in mind the concerns of God, but merely human concerns' (v. 33).

Jesus had spoken plainly. The journey of the Messiah was to death and resurrection, yet we can hardly blame the disciples if they focused on the first part of this statement. They were following Jesus; he was their friend, their teacher, their encourager. The thought of losing him must have been devastating. They could not understand what many even today cannot understand: why did he have to die? They had been looking for someone to defeat the Romans, not be executed by them. The cross sounded like defeat, not victory.

The apostle Paul identified the same problem perhaps 30 years later when he wrote, 'For the message of the cross is foolishness to those who are perishing, but to us who are being saved it is the power of God... we preach Christ crucified: a stumbling block to Jews and foolishness to Gentiles' (1 Corinthians 1:18–23). Douglas Adams was entertaining but wrong when he suggested in *The Hitchhiker's Guide to the Galaxy* that the answer to the ultimate question of life, the universe and everything was 42. It is, in fact, the cross. Sacrificial love.

Prayer

Lord Jesus, thank you that you were obedient to death,
even death on a cross (Philippians 2:8).

STEPHEN RAND

MARK 8:34–37 (TNIV)

Good news: the cross (2)

[Jesus said] 'Whoever wants to be my disciple must deny themselves and take up their cross and follow me. For whoever wants to save their life will lose it, but whoever loses their life for me and for the gospel will save it. What good is it for you to gain the whole world, yet forfeit your soul? Or what can you give in exchange for your soul?'

The disciples had been shocked at the revelation that the Messiah had to die. Even more shocking, perhaps, was this further revelation: they must follow in his footsteps—and those footsteps led resolutely to the shame and pain of public execution.

Jesus had to lose his life so that he could save the world. To receive his sacrifice, however, we have to make the same sacrifice: we have to give up our lives so that they can become his. Paul explained it like this: 'I have been crucified with Christ and it is no longer I who live, but it is Christ who lives in me. And the life I now live in the flesh I live by faith in the Son of God, who loved me and gave himself for me' (Galatians 2:19–20).

This is still a stumbling-block and foolishness to many. It makes no sense. Through my work at Open Doors I am only too aware that for hundreds, possibly thousands, of people each year, this becomes a literal truth. They opt to follow Jesus and they are murdered. Patras Masih was shot dead in India recently. His attackers said they would spare his life if he renounced his faith. 'My son bravely refused,' said his father. 'He clung to Christ and embraced martyrdom.'

For us, the choice is less stark, but the truth is still the same. The good news of the gospel is that the moment we let go of our hold on our own lives, then that is the moment we can receive God's gift of his life. Resurrection life. Eternal life. Life with and in God's presence—here and now and forever.

Reflection

'If Jesus Christ be God and died for me, then no sacrifice can be too great for me to make for him.'

C.T. Studd, England cricketer, then missionary to China, 1860–1931

STEPHEN RAND

Exile

During the 1980s, I was a student in Jerusalem. Someone had suggested to me that, while I was there, I should walk to the top of the Mount of Olives at 4 a.m. to experience the sunrise. What an experience that was—the most beautiful sunrise I have ever seen. As the light hit the Dome of the Rock, built on Mount Moriah, possibly the original site of the temple at the heart of the old city, all I could think of doing was to hum quietly the tune of 'Jerusalem the golden'. I say 'hum the tune quietly' because I was not the only one there. The sunrise was memorable but something else has remained with me during the past 30 years and that was the sight of the young fathers also standing there, holding their babies close to their faces and whispering words (in Hebrew, of course) into their ears. I plucked up courage to ask one of them what was happening and he said, 'I'm telling my son the story'—that is, the story of what it means to be a member of God's chosen people. This reply was to me more powerful than the sunrise and I have never sung 'Jerusalem the Golden' without remembering his words.

Something similar was happening in Babylon at one of the key points in the history of the Jewish people. In 587BC, Jerusalem was destroyed, the temple was ransacked and many of the people were taken in exile to Babylon until about 537BC. The Davidic monarchy came to an end, Judah's political identity was lost, a world of public institutions understood against the backdrop of God's abiding presence disappeared and people began asking deep theological questions about how and why God could have allowed this to happen. It meant an almost total loss of the 'story' that had sustained them for generations. The people had truly become strangers in a strange land.

Over these next two weeks, I want to retrace that exile experience through 14 Bible passages. If being 'strangers in a strange land' defines exile, then, in many ways, we as Christians in the 21st century, in much of the Western world, are also in exile. What lessons can we glean from these Old Testament stories, prophecies and poems about the importance of 'remembering the story' and finding ways 'back home'?

Andrew Jones

DEUTERONOMY 30:15–16 (NRSV)

The consequences of choice

See, I have set before you today life and prosperity, death and adversity. If you obey the commandments of the Lord your God that I am commanding you today, by loving the Lord your God, walking in his ways, and observing his commandments, decrees, and ordinances, then you shall live and become numerous, and the Lord your God will bless you in the land that you are entering to possess.

I vividly remember, as a child, accompanying my parents to the cinema to see *The Ten Commandments*, starring Charlton Heston as Moses. I felt desperately sorry that he was not allowed to enter the promised land after such a long and arduous journey, and I also remember his final plea to the Hebrew people to 'choose life'. That film told the story of one of the defining events in the life of Judaism—Moses leading his people into liberation.

Whoever compiled the book of Deuteronomy—whether it was one person or a group—they clearly had a special interest in the relationship between God and Israel. They knew that those about to enter the promised land needed to do and understand certain things in order to build their relationship with God. As Moses' speech reaches a climax, the form of words recalls earlier covenant encounters (Deuteronomy 32).

The choice that Moses offers is stark: life or death, prosperity or adversity, good or evil, opting for God or no God. For Moses, to opt for God at the centre of life was to accept a great gift, through the sharing of which all the people would prosper. History has shown us that the wrong choice was made and the consequences continued even to the time of exile. The question haunting the people as they entered into exile was 'How could God let this happen to us?' Those ministering to the exiles in Babylon sought to turn the question around and encourage people to ask instead, 'How does God equip us to bear these heavy burdens and what must we do to survive in these new and uncertain times?'

Reflection

'How could God let this happen to us?' It is a question that continues to haunt people today.

ANDREW JONES

2 KINGS 25:8–9, 11–12 (NRSV, ABRIDGED)

Disaster

In the fifth month, on the seventh day of the month—which was the nineteenth year of King Nebuchadnezzar, king of Babylon—Nebuzaradan, the captain of the bodyguard, a servant of the king of Babylon, came to Jerusalem. He burned the house of the Lord, the king's house, and all the houses of Jerusalem; every great house he burned down... [He] carried into exile the rest of the people who were left in the city and the deserters who had defected to the king of Babylon... But [he] left some of the poorest people of the land to be vine-dressers and tillers of the soil.

By the time 1 and 2 Kings were written, religious commentators and prophets were convinced that their rulers had disobeyed God. In both books, the rulers are judged according to their loyal obedience to God and it is shown that national stability depends on this loyalty. Correspondingly, disobedience and idolatry are shown as leading to disaster and crisis. The final part of 2 Kings relates the fall of Judah and Israel and the destruction of Jerusalem by Nebuchadnezzar in 587BC. In July of that year, there was a serious famine and enemy penetration of the city walls, which provoked an attempted flight by Zedekiah the king and his army along the Jordan Valley. The Babylonians stopped them and eliminated any possibility of him resuming royal functions. By August, all was over and a major deportation was underway, with the Babylonians plundering the remaining temple treasures.

This account of the last days of Judah and the beginning of exile makes me wonder what it must have been like for those faithful Jewish people who had not turned away from God. How did they go about planning to maintain their faith in the face of these massive changes? Similarly, over 2500 years later, the question we may want to ask ourselves is: how are we making sense of our own situation of exile, where the church finds itself marginalised more and more in society?

Reflection

Today's verses speak of destruction and of people taken from their places of security. Let us pray for those today who are refugees and far from homes, loved ones and any sense of security.

ANDREW JONES

HABAKKUK 1:2–5 (NRSV, ABRIDGED)

Hard questions

> O Lord, how long shall I cry for help, and you will not listen? Or cry to you 'Violence!' and you will not save?... Destruction and violence are before me; strife and contention arise. So the law becomes slack and justice never prevails... Look at the nations, and see! Be astonished! Be astounded! For a work is being done in your days that you would not believe if you were told.

A major difference between that Babylonian exile and our exile situation today is that, in the sixth century BC, almost everything was interpreted against the backdrop of God's presence and possible intervention. Whether they were faithful or sceptical, everyone had an opinion regarding God. Today, most have forgotten the story of God's involvement in creation and think of him—if at all—as a figure stuck in the past. The prophets of the exile made it their chief concern to continue to 'whisper the story' into the ears of God's children in order to protect their identity, preserve their tradition and help them remember their roots, all of which were under threat.

Habakkuk makes an important and original contribution to Israel's reflections on the nature of God and God's ways with the world. His book begins with a question that he dares to direct to God, raising doubts about divine justice and God's treatment of the wicked. He represents a significant step in attempting to reconcile faith with a breakdown of order and justice—when God seems silent and inactive. Despite the prophet's questions, he remains faithful and trusting.

The lack of theological reflection in our own time reveals our exile mindset. Today, people are uneasy about asking the 'God questions' that the exile prophets asked. Those prophets were certain that believing in a creative, redeeming God meant great care should be taken when viewing the world or loving our fellow humans; it is all connected.

Reflection

God may well be saying to us, 'Look... and see! Be astonished! Be astounded! Yes, there is destruction and horror in many parts of the world today, but there is also beauty and love, usually in everyday simple things.' As we encounter them, let us give thanks to God and rejoice.

ANDREW JONES

LAMENTATIONS 1:1, 3 (NRSV)

Weeping in the ruins

How lonely sits the city that once was full of people! How like a widow she has become, she that was great among the nations! She that was a princess among the provinces has become a vassal… Judah has gone into exile with suffering and hard servitude; she lives now among the nations, and finds no resting place; her pursuers have all overtaken her in the midst of her distress.

This must be the most depressingly titled of all the biblical books! Originally it was a scroll of five poems designed to be read at the solemn commemoration of the destruction of the temple. The author (or authors) used the language of bereavement to assist the exiles in their remembrance of catastrophic loss. The exile brought everything they thought they knew about God into serious question—the inconceivable had happened and now they could only lament.

People have a habit of asking the same questions again and again. Where I live, local people ask every summer, 'When will the visitors leave so that we can find a place to park?' In an exile situation, profoundly troubling questions recur. How can God let this happen? How can those of us who are faithful make sense of God in these events? How will faith be possible in the future?

In Hebrew, the title of Lamentations is 'Ekah'—literally, 'How'. The opening verses reveal the tragic reversal of fortune experienced by Israel. Once full of people, the centre of attention, Jerusalem finds herself sitting alone—a widow, whose social status means she is open to mistreatment because she lacks protection. One of the main refrains of the book is the absence of consolation. It is as if those observing the bereavement simply say, 'Well, you were warned!'

That is how life in Babylon began for the exiles, but despite the mournful nature of most of Lamentations, there is also a real note of trust in God and hope for the future.

Reflection

We may find ourselves in situations of bitter bereavement—and the challenge is to hold on to trust in God and hope, knowing that this has sustained so many who have journeyed before us.

ANDREW JONES

LAMENTATIONS 5:19–22 (NRSV)

Keeping hope alive

> But you, O Lord, reign for ever; your throne endures to all generations. Why have you forgotten us completely? Why have you forsaken us these many days? Restore us to yourself, O Lord, that we may be restored; renew our days as of old—unless you have utterly rejected us, and are angry with us beyond measure.

Whoever wrote Lamentations, one thing is clear—they were accomplished in the art of poetry. The laments follow a strict and ancient pattern. The first four poems are 'acrostic'—that is, each line or series of lines begins with successive letters of the Hebrew alphabet. The fifth poem (part of which forms today's passage) has, instead, 22 lines—the number of letters in the Hebrew alphabet. Possibly this pattern was an aid to memory (as in Psalm 119), a way of symbolising completeness (A to Z) or an act of devotion similar to the rosary or the Jesus Prayer, involving a degree of repetition.

Towards the end of this final poem, the collapse of social and religious order is complete. Jerusalem and the temple have been destroyed and the people are forced to ask whether this means that God himself is also dead. Our verses are a categorical '*no*' to that question. The author encourages the people to see that God is not dead and that as long as they can believe this, hope will remain alive.

Here we also find the recurring question 'Why?' But here it is not so much asking 'Why has this happened?'—the people know that by now—but more 'How long will this last?' At the end, the great lamentation fades away not with a cry for revenge or cheap optimism but with a deep prayer of repentance and a sober recognition of the facts. At last, the people are beginning to see that they should be less concerned with blaming everyone else and more concerned with examining their own role in the crisis. That hits such a contemporary note...

Reflection

Taking responsibility or admitting that we have at least a shared responsibility for things that happen around us is often challenging. It is an essential part of the Christian life, however, and, from the outset, Christians have been called to 'repent'.

ANDREW JONES

JEREMIAH 4:8–9, 11–12 (NRSV)

Converting the heart

Put on sackcloth, lament and wail: 'The fierce anger of the Lord has not turned away from us.' On that day, says the Lord, courage shall fail the king and the officials; the priests shall be appalled and the prophets astounded... At that time it will be said to this people and to Jerusalem: A hot wind comes from me out of the bare heights in the desert toward my poor people, not to winnow or cleanse—a wind too strong for that. Now it is I who speak in judgment against them.

With some understanding of the significance and events of the exile, we can begin to see which of the prophets prepared the people for the crisis of destruction and deportation, which ones lived with and ministered to them in exile and which prepared them for the journey home.

Jeremiah lived during the latter part of the seventh century and first part of the sixth century BC. He was one of those preparing the people for the impending devastation. Repeatedly, he warned of the coming catastrophe, and he lived to see this prediction come true with the fall of Jerusalem. Interestingly, he also foretold the eventual return of the people from exile and the restoration of the nation.

We get the impression that Jeremiah was a sensitive and caring pastor who loved his people enormously. He found it difficult to be judgmental and, time and again, he preached with deep emotion about his own sufferings and the challenges he faced as a prophet. Today's passage comes from such a context. It is clearly part of a longer poem (vv. 3–31) in which Jeremiah begs the people once and for all to repent, suggesting that the hidden feelings of the heart are actually more important than exterior demonstrations. He calls for a new conversion—not so much the restoration of long-neglected religious practices as a conversion of the heart—and he talks of sackcloth as a personal garment of mourning.

Reflection

Too often we may talk of 'conversion' or a 'return to traditional values' as if that applies only to 'those people over there'. We forget that the peace of the world, indeed the conversion of the world, begins with us.

ANDREW JONES

Saturday 30 June

JEREMIAH 36:1–3 (NRSV, ABRIDGED)

If only

> In the fourth year of King Jehoiakim... this word came to Jeremiah from the Lord: Take a scroll and write on it all the words that I have spoken to you against Israel and Judah and all the nations, from the day I spoke to you, from the days of Josiah until today. It may be that when the house of Judah hears of all the disasters that I intend to do to them, all of them may turn from their evil ways, so that I may forgive their iniquity and their sin.

The prophets were only too aware of the ancient religious traditions of Israel and the significance of the 'covenant'. Many of them were unhappy with how those traditions had been interpreted in the life of the nation. Too often it was a subjective interpretation—covenant on my terms and in the way that suits me (times have not changed). Jeremiah was one of those who criticised this subjectivism. He and others set about writing a history of Israel, showing that the question 'How could God let this happen?' had an uncomfortably easy answer. It was the people's fault or, more specifically, the fault of the leaders of Israel. The prophets set out a kind of constitution that described what the nation would be like if people took the covenant seriously. Was this not precisely what Moses was trying to do in that final speech towards the end of Deuteronomy?

Today's verses are some of the most photographic of Jeremiah's many vivid pictures. The 'scroll' probably refers to long strips of papyrus sheets or skins sewn together. It was to contain all Jeremiah's sayings since God had called him to be a prophet. My reading of the passage is that God is saying, 'if only...'—if only the people could see what they are doing; if only they could see where all this will lead; if only they could remember the past... Maybe then their hearts would change and they would begin to find their way home.

Reflection

Yesterday we paused to think of the importance of being a repentant people. Today's passage shows that truly accepting that God can forgive—and accepting God's forgiveness as both grace and gift—can change lives.

ANDREW JONES

PSALM 137:1–4 (NRSV)

In a strange land

By the rivers of Babylon—there we sat down and there we wept when we remembered Zion. On the willows there we hung up our harps. For there our captors asked us for songs, and our tormentors asked for mirth, saying, 'Sing us one of the songs of Zion!' How could we sing the Lord's song in a foreign land?

This psalm, more than any other writing from the exile, captures the people's homesickness and despondency. The oath never to forget Jerusalem (vv. 5–6) suggests that the authors are well and truly in the throes of captivity. Interestingly, the use of past tenses in Jewish poetry of lament indicates that the distress is happening there and then. When we read this psalm, then, we are reading actual words once uttered by despairing and angry people forced to dwell in a foreign land.

Two things stand out here: the water and the music. There is a vivid reference to the great rivers and canals of Babylon. These would have struck the captives powerfully by contrast with the mountains of home, whose streams only filled at rare times of rain. Then the Babylonians call on them to sing, not necessarily with malice but because, in those days, Israel was noted for its music. They could not sing, though, either because that foreign land was ritually unclean and not fit for music (Amos 7; Ezekiel 4) or, more likely, because they were too distressed.

For the people of the three great faiths of Abraham—Judaism, Christianity, Islam—Jerusalem continues to be a spiritual home. Today, these verses can be an expression of concern for that troubled city, where Christians are a minority among Jews and Muslims; where Jews who have sought refuge there encounter hatred; where Muslims are forced to live on the margins, fighting for recognition. We should all feel a special responsibility towards the people of Jerusalem and pray for resolution of all that causes those living there to feel like strangers in a strange land.

Reflection

When I was a student in Jerusalem, I became convinced that the psalmist was right to ask us to pray for the peace of Jerusalem. Let's all do that today.

ANDREW JONES

New covenant

> The days are surely coming, says the Lord, when I will make a new covenant with the house of Israel and the house of Judah. It will not be like the covenant that I made with their ancestors when I took them by the hand to bring them out of the land of Egypt—a covenant that they broke, though I was their husband, says the Lord… I will put my law within them, and I will write it on their hearts; and I will be their God, and they shall be my people.

The prophets lived at a time of great crisis and it was natural that much of what they proclaimed was tinged with bitterness. One can imagine only too well the quarrelling within and between the nations under the shadow of that great exile. Jeremiah's ministry was in direct response to this sense of crisis and desperation, when the spiritual life of the people was generally in tatters.

Jeremiah's ministry during exile was mainly concerned with consoling the people. There is a real profundity about this passage and its sound of consolation. I believe this is the only Old Testament passage that mentions the 'new covenant'. Jeremiah movingly compares this so-called new covenant with the one made on Sinai, but this one has a sense of being universal: God is now keen to establish a lasting relationship with all people.

One of the greatest spiritual writers of the 20th century, Thomas Merton, once said that the most urgent task facing the contemporary church was not survival but prophecy. Our contemporary exile situation presents us with immense and complex challenges, not least in trying to live authentic lives in a world that is ripped by human greed and selfishness. Many are looking for new ways of being faithful to the God who, through covenant, shares our lives. A prophetic church is one that is open to facing the big issues head-on in the name of the one who stands at the heart of that covenant, Jesus Christ, who himself continues to be for us liberation, acceptance, compassion, forgiveness and love.

Reflection

A prophetic challenge for us today is how to be liberation, acceptance, compassion, forgiveness and love for one another.

ANDREW JONES

EZEKIEL 11:17–20 (NRSV, ABRIDGED)

A different outlook

Thus says the Lord God: I will gather you from the peoples, and assemble you out of the countries where you have been scattered, and I will give you the land of Israel. When they come there, they will remove from it all its detestable things... I will give them one heart, and put a new spirit within them; I will remove the heart of stone from their flesh and give them a heart of flesh, so that they may follow my statutes and keep my ordinances... Then they shall be my people, and I will be their God.

Around 539BC, the Babylonian empire was conquered by the Persians. The exiles' circumstances began to change and the possibility emerged of returning home. It was probably then that the prophets' message changed from blame and repentance to hope for the future.

Exile had changed the people's outlook. They had come to understand that God was not just the best of many gods whose influence only extended to Israel's borders. He was in fact the only God and this brought new challenges. If God was the only God, then he was God of all creation, all history and, most importantly, all peoples. Writers such as Ezekiel—a man of deep faith who emphasised the need for renewal of the heart and the responsibility of everyone for their own sins—grappled with these new understandings.

In our passage, the prophet dreams about stony hearts becoming generous and loving, but some commentators prefer to explain this in terms of having one heart or a single-minded heart. If so, Ezekiel is calling for the people to become unified in their loyalty to God instead of unable to decide which way to go—in the direction of God or the idols. I warm to that interpretation. In the context of the exile, it could be understood as a warning: when you get home, for goodness sake *be united*!

Reflection

In our dealings with one another, it is often far too easy to nurture a heart of stone. Let us work hard to discover our hearts of flesh—the kind and generous approach—but also, as Christians, let us strive to speak as one united family.

ANDREW JONES

ISAIAH 40:1–3 (NRSV)

Getting ready for return

Comfort, O comfort my people, says your God. Speak tenderly to Jerusalem, and cry to her that she has served her term, that her penalty is paid, that she has received from the Lord's hand double for all her sins. A voice cries out: 'In the wilderness prepare the way of the Lord, make straight in the desert a highway for our God.'

One of the books in the Bible that I most enjoyed studying at university and with my parish study group was Isaiah. It covers the whole of the exilic period, with chapters 1—39 covering the period when Judah was threatened by Assyria and a national crisis seemed likely. Isaiah, however, proclaims that the greatest threat is not foreign might but the fact that the people are turning away from God. By chapters 40—55, that crisis has come in the form of exile, but the prophet announces the people will soon return home—liberation is at hand. The third section addresses the people following the return, when the prophet reassures them that God will be faithful to his promises, but expects their trust.

Our passage today comes from the middle period, when Isaiah begins to prepare the people for not only a literal journey home but also a brand new kind of life following years of being crushed into hopelessness. It opens with a tone of great mercy where God does not simply offer 'comfort' but also reassures the people about the covenant that has historically bonded them to him. Jerusalem here is not a place but, rather, the actual people in exile.

To read on beyond these verses is to see that the return home will mean the people will never be the same again. Indeed, the return from exile will be to see and even feel the 'glory of the Lord' (v. 5). None of us, when we leave a place of desolation or of turmoil, is ever the same as we once were. To be no longer strangers in a strange land brings 'comfort', yes, but it reveals 'God's glory', too.

Reflection

To begin the day with prayer is to discover anew the compass that will lead us home throughout that day—and tomorrow, to discover it again.

ANDREW JONES

ISAIAH 40:28–31 (NRSV)

Between two worlds

Have you not known? Have you not heard? The Lord is the everlasting God, the Creator of the ends of the earth. He does not faint or grow weary; his understanding is unsearchable. He gives power to the faint, and strengthens the powerless. Even youths will faint and be weary, and the young will fall exhausted; but those who wait for the Lord shall renew their strength, they shall mount up with wings like eagles, they shall run and not be weary, they shall walk and not faint.

Reading Isaiah 40 reminds me of the liturgical season of Advent. This is not only because many of the Old Testament readings for Advent come from Isaiah but also because the book (or at least chapters 40—55) are associated with themes of hope, preparation and waiting. In our final verses here, Isaiah provides an excellent description of faith, in a way typical of Old Testament thinking, as 'waiting for the Lord' (v. 31)—a phrase capturing that exilic sense of helplessness and a deepening appreciation of God's redeeming power.

Some of the most profound encounters found in the Bible come in what I call 'waiting moments', times of retreat or withdrawal. There are many biblical examples—Jesus in the wilderness, Jesus and his three disciples at the transfiguration, the upper room, the garden of Gethsemane, the disciples after the crucifixion, to name but a few.

Advent is a time to 'wait' patiently, a point in our Christian year when we stand between two worlds, as if in exile, before emerging from that waiting exile at Christmas. In one world, the Christ-child hides in Mary's womb—a shadow, a secret—and, in the other, God's great act of incarnation bursts upon us to lead us home. Like the exiles of old, will we heed Isaiah's proclamation that 'the Lord is the everlasting God' and will we choose to enter the world of the newborn child, who will inevitably bring challenge but trust and hope as well?

Reflection

Through our encounter with Christ today, may we have the strength and courage to fly like eagles or run like athletes or maybe just to walk calmly, but always in God's strength.

ANDREW JONES

Ezra 1:2–3 (NRSV)

Rebuilding identity

'Thus says King Cyrus of Persia: The Lord, the God of heaven, has given me all the kingdoms of the earth, and he has charged me to build him a house at Jerusalem in Judah. Any of those among you who are of his people—may their God be with them!—are now permitted to go up to Jerusalem in Judah, and rebuild the house of the Lord, the God of Israel—he is the God who is in Jerusalem.'

The book of Ezra is usually dated to around 458BC and opens with the decree allowing the Jews to return to Jerusalem and Cyrus' invitation to rebuild the temple. In truth, the majority of the descendants of the original exiles did *not* return. We can easily imagine how, well over a generation later, many had settled in Babylon, intermarried and integrated. They had started a new life, albeit originally reluctantly and in a state of depression.

Realistically, then, it was probably a minority who returned and these people set strict rules on social life so as to define who was really Jewish and who was not. In that sense, the book of Ezra essentially describes the efforts of a group under threat to maintain identity or even rebrand themselves in a way which was sustainable but also faithful to the received tradition. Israel entered the exile as a holy nation but emerged from it, according to Ezra, as a holy people, a holy community or, possibly, even a holy minority.

Whatever the actual circumstances, this was certainly a most formative and defining time. They started to build what is known as 'the Second Temple', which was eventually completed by Herod the Great; this was the one in which Jesus was active. Some of the remaining stones are part of what Jews until recently called the 'Wailing Wall' and now the 'Western Wall'. It marks a site that Jews and Muslims continue to hold in high regard and we can pray and hope that it may be a place where peace may be finally sorted out.

Reflection

Ruins and buildings are often rebuilt before they completely fall down and disappear. Similarly, relationships can be rebuilt and so can our own personal lives.

Andrew Jones

EZRA 6:19–20, 22 (NRSV, ABRIDGED)

On with the journey

On the fourteenth day of the first month the returned exiles kept the Passover. For both the priests and the Levites had purified themselves... So they killed the Passover lamb for all the returned exiles, for their fellow priests, and for themselves... With joy they celebrated the festival of unleavened bread for seven days; for the Lord had made them joyful, and had turned the heart of the king of Assyria to them, so that he aided them in the work on the house of God.

We began these readings with Moses' speech offering a choice between a good life in obedience to God and a very different kind of life in opposition to God. Although the people chose badly, the ever-loving God offered them another chance, this time through the horrors of exile. We end with a passage reminding us of the night before the exodus, when God laid down the ordinances for the first Passover (Exodus 12:43–51). The temple is near completion and the people are about to dedicate it to God—and they celebrate the Passover, their ceremony of identity.

So how does the story of the exile challenge us today? This is an essential question—otherwise it remains a history lesson with no contemporary meaning. We have seen how a people became distracted from God's ways and ended up in crisis. Out of this crisis emerged opportunities to think about God differently and, ultimately, the people returned home, refreshed and renewed.

To feel we have faith neatly sewn up means we miss the whole point of what the Jews learnt in Babylon about themselves, life and God. For us as Christians, finding our way home from exile is a journey that started in God before we were born and will end only when we find ourselves back in God's presence. Our challenge is to keep spotting God as he reveals himself to us along the way and be ready to greet him—perhaps in the most unlikely of places and the most surprising of people.

Prayer

Lord, help me to spot you in all those places and people you choose to reveal yourself to me through today, but first give me the grace to listen attentively and watch carefully.

ANDREW JONES

The God of Abraham

Over the next two weeks, we are looking at the familiar story of Abraham. The details will not concern us so much as what his life reveals about his relationship with God and his understanding of the God he worshipped.

Abraham grew up with no knowledge of the true and living God. The members of his family were idol worshippers in the Sumerian city of Ur of the Chaldees. Only when the God of glory appeared to him did he develop any first-hand knowledge of the real God.

Abraham had no scriptures to guide him, no people to call on to advise him, no tradition by which to navigate his way. He was beginning from scratch and everything he learned about God he discovered through lived experience.

The story of Abraham, then, is like an unfolding picture of God. Through the events and circumstances of his life, God is gradually revealing himself not just to Abraham but also to the world. In particular, Abraham begins to learn the names of God. Each name reveals a facet of God's identity and, as we journey with Abraham, we, too, will begin to learn his names, understand his character and become familiar with his ways.

God speaks to Abraham in many different ways and he is able to recognise the divine voice. He is called to a life of faith and obedience as he follows God's leading and awaits the fulfilment of the promises God makes to him. Sometimes he is strong in faith, sometimes he is weak; often he is a shining example, sometimes a bad one. Always he is human, an ordinary man doing his best to live his life in fellowship with the God who has taken hold of his life.

Therein lies the benefit for us of musing on his life. Abraham is called 'the man of faith' (Galatians 3:9), 'God's friend' (James 2:23) and 'the father of all who believe' (Romans 4:11). As we walk with him and listen to his life, something of his passion for God will surely rub off on us and, with the help of the Holy Spirit, we, too, will be enabled to develop a life of intimacy with God.

Tony Horsfall

ACTS 7:2–4 (NIV)

'The God of glory'

[Stephen said] 'Brothers and fathers, listen to me! The God of glory appeared to our father Abraham while he was still in Mesopotamia, before he lived in Haran. "Leave your country and your people," God said, "and go to the land I will show you." So he left the land of the Chaldeans and settled in Haran. After the death of his father, God sent him to this land where you are now living.'

Stephen's speech before the Sanhedrin represents a masterful summary of the Old Testament and a glimpse into the beginning of Abraham's faith. The point of origin was an unlikely place—the mighty Chaldean city of Ur (Genesis 11:28; Nehemiah 9:7), home to the giant ziggurat where the god Nannar was worshipped in golden splendour.

Abraham's heart was never satisfied by the worship of man-made deities, however splendid, and he longed for something more. Then one day he encountered the true and living God, the God of glory, whose presence overwhelmed him and captured his devotion. We are not told how God appeared to him. Was it in a dream or a vision? Was it a moment of dramatic encounter or a gradual dawning of awareness? Whatever happened, Abraham was left in no doubt about the existence of a God far more glorious that Nannar or any other Chaldean deity (Joshua 24:2–3).

Man-made deities derive their glory from external things, like gold and silver—something given to them by craftsmen—but the glory of the true God is an internal quality, derived from his uncreated being, inherent within himself. He is One who is holy and pure, majestic and awesome, whose presence is brighter than the shining sun. Mostly, his glory is veiled for it is too intense for human eyes (1 Timothy 6:16), but on this occasion, to leave Abraham in no doubt as to which deity to follow, God allowed his splendour to shine through.

With the revelation of God's glory comes a summons to follow and, for Abraham, a life of pilgrimage begins.

Prayer

Lord, so many glittering deities call for my allegiance. May I have an awareness of your glory, so I am in no doubt whom to follow.

TONY HORSFALL

Genesis 12:1–4 (NIV)

The God who calls

The Lord had said to Abram, 'Leave your country, your people and your father's household and go to the land I will show you. I will make you into a great nation and I will bless you; I will make your name great, and you will be a blessing. I will bless those who bless you, and whoever curses you I will curse; and all peoples on earth will be blessed through you.' So Abram left, as the Lord had told him.

The summons of God that Abram (as he was then known) received in Ur resulted in the family moving to Haran, where they settled until the demise of Abram's father, Terah (11:27–32). His death seems to have liberated Abram to set out again on the path of obedience.

Abram then becomes aware that the appearance of God was not by accident but by design and a divine plan has been set in motion in which he will play a key part. God is the initiator, but he is called to respond. First, there is the making of a promise: God will bless Abram, make his name great and multiply him into a great nation. Second, there is a guarantee of protection: God will watch over him on his journey. Third, there is a statement of purpose: the whole earth will be blessed as a result of his obedience.

Did Abram understand the destiny that was placed before him? I doubt it, for there is too much to take in. What is clear, though, is that he recognises the voice of God and acts accordingly, confidently setting out with his family on his great adventure of faith, even though the details remain sketchy.

Abram is the prototype for all who desire to follow God's will. The general outline remains the same. God blesses us in order that we may become a blessing to others. His goodness comes to us not as an end in itself, but so that we may share it generously with others and always with a global application.

Prayer

Lord, you have blessed me with so much. May I willingly use what I have for your glory and the blessing of others.

Tony Horsfall

GENESIS 12:6–8 (NIV)

Worthy to be worshipped

Abram travelled through the land as far as the site of the great tree of Moreh at Shechem. At that time the Canaanites were in the land. The Lord appeared to Abram and said, 'To your offspring I will give this land.' So he built an altar there to the Lord, who had appeared to him. From there he went on towards the hills east of Bethel and pitched his tent, with Bethel on the west and Ai on the east. There he built an altar to the Lord and called on the name of the Lord.

As Abram travels onwards, his certainty in the promise of God may have been undermined by the presence of the Canaanites. They would not simply give up their land to these wandering strangers and Abram's faith might have wavered—how would God bring his purposes to pass?

In order to strengthen him, the Lord appears to Abram again, confirming his intention to give this particular land to his offspring, regardless of contrary appearances. This reassurance affects him deeply and, in response, he builds an altar to the Lord—his first tangible expression of worship. The altar was probably little more than a heap of stones, with perhaps the possibility of offering sacrifice, but its significance was mostly as a 'marker'—a genuine expression of his connection with God, a practical way of giving thanks and a visible reminder of his commitment to do his will.

Moving further on, Abram finds a more suitable resting place, between Bethel and Ai, where he pitches his tent. Here he builds a second altar and calls on the name of the Lord. This represents his first faltering steps in prayer—the calling out to God for help on the basis of his name or character.

Worship and prayer thus mark the early steps of Abram's faith journey and reflect his growing relationship with God. The One he is getting to know is worthy to be worshipped and great enough to be turned to in time of need.

Prayer

Lord, thank you that it is possible to know you in a personal way.
May I, too, grow in worship and in prayer.

TONY HORSFALL

GENESIS 14:17–20 (NIV)

'God Most High'

After Abram returned from defeating Kedorlaomer and the kings allied with him, the king of Sodom came out to meet him in the Valley of Shaveh (that is, the King's Valley). Then Melchizedek king of Salem brought out bread and wine. He was priest of God Most High, and he blessed Abram, saying, 'Blessed be Abram by God Most High, Creator of heaven and earth. And blessed be God Most High, who delivered your enemies into your hand.' Then Abram gave him a tenth of everything.

Although Abram and his nephew Lot have chosen to go their separate ways, when Lot and the people of Sodom are attacked it is Abram who rescues them. Returning victorious from battle, he encounters the mysterious Melchizedek, king of Salem and priest of the Most High God.

Hebrews (7:1–19) interprets Melchizedek as a picture of Christ, who, it is said, is a priest after the order of Melchizedek—that is, one not specifically descended from the priestly line of Levi. While this is an interesting line of thought, our concern here is to understand the insight that Melchizedek brings to Abram about the Most High God.

In the context of a simple meal, Melchizedek gives Abram a priestly blessing. The Creator God is higher in rank and power than any so-called deity. He is El-Elyon, the Most High God, unrivalled, unequalled and incomparable. Canaanite deities were often ranked according to their importance, but Abram's God is high over them all.

This exalted God has demonstrated his supremacy by giving Abram victory over his enemies. It is therefore appropriate that Abram should join in praising him for such a gracious deliverance. The giving of a tenth of the spoils of war is an act of gratitude on Abram's part, freely offered as an act of worship. This whole encounter serves to enlarge Abram's understanding of the greatness of God. This is no tribal deity to be ranked alongside rival gods; he is supreme over all and is to be exalted in the lives of his followers.

Prayer

'For you, O Lord, are the Most High over all the earth;
you are exalted far above all gods' (Psalm 97:9).

TONY HORSFALL

GENESIS 15:1–4 (NIV)

'I am your shield'

After this, the word of the Lord came to Abram in a vision: 'Do not be afraid, Abram. I am your shield, your very great reward.' But Abram said, 'O Sovereign Lord, what can you give me since I remain childless and the one who will inherit my estate is Eliezer of Damascus?' And Abram said, 'You have given me no children; so a servant in my household will be my heir.' Then the word of the Lord came to him: 'This man will not be your heir, but a son coming from your own body will be your heir.'

For the first time, we are told how God spoke to Abram. This time it is in a vision. Having just been involved in a fierce battle, the idea that God was his shield would have been a familiar and understandable image and welcome news to Abram. Many fears still crowded his mind, so the reassurance that God would protect him fortified his soul.

As well as being a shield, the Lord reveals to Abram that he is also his reward. This can be understood in two ways. First, that knowing God is the most important thing and is the reward of his obedience. Second, that God will reward his obedience in some tangible way. While both are true, Abram seems to have taken the second meaning and raises the issue of a child and heir.

Abram's growing relationship with God is evidenced in the dialogue that follows. He has no hesitation in speaking to God about what concerns him most. Both he and Sarah are advanced in years and childless. Their servant Eliezer stands to inherit everything, but he is not family. Where, then, is God's promise of offspring? A strong relationship is based on honesty and speaking the truth and a relationship with God is no different. We, too, need to have the confidence to be real with God.

Again God speaks—perhaps this time directly into his soul—with clarity and conviction. The promise of God is still true. He will have a son and that son will be his own flesh and blood.

Prayer

God, you are my shield and everything I need.

TONY HORSFALL

GENESIS 15:8–9, 18–21 (NIV)

The covenant-keeping God

Abram said, 'O Sovereign Lord, how can I know that I will gain possession of it?' So the Lord said to him, 'Bring me a heifer, a goat and a ram, each three years old, along with a dove and a young pigeon.'... On that day the Lord made a covenant with Abram and said, 'To your descendants I give this land, from the river of Egypt to the great river, the Euphrates—the land of the Kenites, Kenizzites, Kadmonites, Hittites, Perizzites, Rephaites, Amorites, Canaanites, Girgashites and Jebusites.'

The uncertainty that Abram felt over the gift of a son is now expressed with regard to the promise of land. 'How can I be sure?' is the essence of his question, since the land is already inhabited and there is, as yet, no indication of anything changing.

To ensure that Abram is left in no doubt concerning his purposes, the Lord makes a formal covenant with him in a ritual that seems strange to us, but then was full of meaning. A covenant is a binding agreement between two parties, clearly stating plans and expectations. Earlier, God made promises to Abram, and he now underlines his intention to fulfil every one of them by formalising them in a covenant.

This is a blood covenant, authenticated by sacrifice (vv. 10–11). Normally the two parties involved would walk between the divided halves of animals, symbolically pledging their own lives if they should violate the terms of the agreement. Here, only God walks between them, for this is his covenant, and the promises he makes are unconditional; he will keep his word whether Abram deserves it or not.

We should not underestimate the positive impact that this had on Abram's faith. It was a pivotal moment in his evolving relationship with God. Now he knows God can be trusted and that, no matter how long it takes (vv. 13–16), the promises will come to fruition. He can continue to follow the leading of God with confidence and assurance.

God remains faithful to every promise he has made and his utter reliability is the bedrock for our faith as well.

Prayer

Lord, today I place my faith in your faithfulness.

TONY HORSFALL

GENESIS 16:7–9, 13 (NIV)

The 'God who sees me'

The angel of the Lord found Hagar near a spring in the desert; it was the spring that is beside the road to Shur. And he said, 'Hagar, servant of Sarai, where have you come from, and where are you going?' 'I'm running away from my mistress Sarai,' she answered. Then the angel of the Lord told her, 'Go back to your mistress and submit to her.'... [Hagar] gave this name to the Lord who spoke to her: 'You are the God who sees me,' for she said, 'I have now seen the One who sees me.'

In her impatience to have a child, Sarai had encouraged Abram to sleep with her maidservant, Hagar. When a child was conceived and Hagar became boastful, Sarai harshly ill-treated her so that she was forced to flee.

Here we find Hagar alone, impoverished, pregnant and wandering in the desert. How despondent she must have felt! What a sense of abandonment must have gripped her soul. There is no one to care for her, no one to support her at her most vulnerable moment.

Yet she is not alone, for God is aware of her. He knows what she has suffered and has compassion for her predicament. The angel of the Lord finds her in the desert and gently coaxes her to return. His presence and reassurance give her hope that she will be well received and there is a future for her child.

Hagar's experience provides her with an amazing insight into the character of God: 'You are the God who sees me' (v. 13). Her adversity has created the context for a new revelation of God—one who is aware of our circumstances, who knows our history, whose watchful eye is always upon us.

If, today, you find yourself in a desolate place, if circumstances seem to be against you, if you feel as if no one cares for you, remember this: God is the One who sees you and will come to you. He is always near and will help you to find a way through your troubles. Listen for his reassuring voice.

Prayer

Lord, your eye is on the sparrow and you are watching over me as well.

TONY HORSFALL

GENESIS 17:1–5 (NIV)

'God Almighty'

When Abram was ninety-nine years old, the Lord appeared to him and said, 'I am God Almighty; walk before me and be blameless. I will confirm my covenant between me and you and will greatly increase your numbers.' Abram fell face down, and God said to him, 'As for me, this is my covenant with you: you will be the father of many nations. No longer will you be called Abram; your name will be Abraham, for I have made you a father of many nations.'

Some 13 silent years pass following the birth of Ishmael to Hagar, during which time Abram is purified of impatience and impulsiveness and learns to wait for the Lord. He is 99 years old when God speaks again. God is never in a hurry and his timing is always perfect.

The new word from God brings a fresh revelation of God as the Almighty One (El Shaddai). Not only is he gracious in making promises and faithful enough to keep them but he is also powerful enough to bring them to pass, no matter what the obstacles may be. He will certainly keep his covenant with Abram.

This is also a moment of transformation, signified in the giving of a new name. No longer will he be called Abram ('exalted father') but, instead, from now on he will be Abraham ('father of many'), reflecting more accurately the purpose God has for him. This is a change that the Almighty will bring about, for it is not within Abram's power to achieve, as he well knows by now. In accepting his new name, he will be making space within his life for the Almighty to do his gracious work. He will at last be accepting his destiny.

The 'name' we go by (or the 'label' other people put on us) can profoundly influence how we perceive ourselves. If we think we are 'stupid', 'useless' or 'no good', we may well be locked into a low expectation of what we can achieve in life. If we accept the words of the Almighty—'beloved', 'chosen', 'forgiven'—then we, too, can fulfil our God-given destiny.

Prayer

Almighty God, let me see my potential in you.

TONY HORSFALL

GENESIS 18:1–3 (NIV)

Three in one

The Lord appeared to Abraham near the great trees of Mamre while he was sitting at the entrance to his tent in the heat of the day. Abraham looked up and saw three men standing nearby. When he saw them, he hurried from the entrance of his tent to meet them and bowed low to the ground. He said, 'If I have found favour in your eyes, my lord, do not pass your servant by.'

This incident in the life of Abraham is often associated with Rublev's icon of the Holy Trinity, painted in 1410. Rublev was in no doubt that these were divine visitors and used the imagery to depict the mystery of God as three in one.

For Abraham, what began as an ordinary day turned into something very special. Perhaps he was dozing after lunch (on a very hot afternoon) when three men appeared suddenly at his tent. Something about their bearing suggested they were important and his response was to bow humbly before them. Being hospitable, he invited them into his tent for refreshment and food. After they had eaten, they delivered their message: about that time the following year, Sarah would have a son (v. 10). Nothing is impossible for Almighty God. Not even advanced age and barrenness will limit God's creative power.

Although Abraham sees three men approaching, he greets them as one: 'If I have found favour in your eyes, my lord' (v. 3), he says. Further, the expression 'Then the Lord said' is used several times (vv. 10, 13, 17, 20, 26), as if they are speaking with one divine voice. By the time the men leave, Abraham is in no doubt that he has met with God (v. 33).

The doctrine of the Trinity is one of the great mysteries of the Christian faith. It is the belief that, although God is one, he has revealed himself in three distinct persons—Father, Son and Holy Spirit. The doctrine is never explicitly stated in scripture, but passages like this force us to come to the conclusion that this must be so. Human intellect will never fathom the Almighty. We must be comfortable with mystery.

Prayer

Lord, do not pass your servant by.

TONY HORSFALL

GENESIS 18:22–25 (NIV)

The 'Judge of all the earth'

> The men turned away and went towards Sodom, but Abraham remained standing before the Lord. Then Abraham approached him and said: 'Will you sweep away the righteous with the wicked? What if there are fifty righteous people in the city? Will you really sweep it away and not spare the place for the sake of the fifty righteous people in it? Far be it from you to do such a thing—to kill the righteous with the wicked, treating the righteous and the wicked alike. Far be it from you! Will not the Judge of all the earth do right?'

As we have already noted, scripture calls Abraham the friend of God (Isaiah 41:8; James 2:23). The divine disclosure in our passage concerning the impending judgment of Sodom reflects the depth of the relationship he now enjoys with the Lord, who did not want to hide from his servant what was about to happen.

Once again, Abraham comes to the rescue of Sodom—probably with the fate of Lot and his family in his mind. Conscious of his own humanity and the danger of seeming to be presumptuous, Abraham daringly asks that the city might be spared if righteous people can be found within. There follows a period of intense 'negotiation' as Abraham intercedes before God in the hope that Sodom might be reprieved.

Abraham's case is built around his knowledge of God. Yes, he is the Judge of all the earth and, as Creator, has the right to set the standards and punish wickedness, but Abraham is also aware that God is just and will not act unfairly. He believes that God will not allow the righteous (if there are any) to perish along with the wicked. This provides hope for Lot's salvation.

Abraham's brave imploring of God is the inspiration for much intercessory prayer—that is, prayer offered on behalf of others who cannot or will not pray for themselves. It often finds its motivation in the desire for others to be spared the judgment of God and derives its confidence from the knowledge that, although God is judge, he will always do that which is right.

Reflection

Shall not the Judge of all the earth do right?

TONY HORSFALL

GENESIS 21:1–5 (NIV)

God of grace

Now the Lord was gracious to Sarah as he had said, and the Lord did for Sarah what he had promised. Sarah became pregnant and bore a son to Abraham in his old age, at the very time God had promised him. Abraham gave the name Isaac to the son Sarah bore him. When his son Isaac was eight days old, Abraham circumcised him, as God commanded him. Abraham was a hundred years old when his son Isaac was born to him.

The word 'grace' has not been mentioned so far in the story of Abraham, but it is present throughout as the underlying reason for the blessing that attends his life. Grace is the notion that God chooses to do good to us even though we have done nothing to merit it and despite all which would disqualify us. It is for this reason that grace is often defined as 'God's undeserved favour'.

The most tangible expression of grace at work in the lives of Abraham and Sarah is in the gift of a child of their own. Their faith in God's promise had often wavered, despite repeated reassurances, and Sarah's behaviour with Hagar hardly commended her. She had laughed in unbelief at the message of the three visitors (18:12), so when she eventually became pregnant, it was all to do with God's grace towards her.

Everything about the birth has the hallmarks of divine activity. The parents are well past the age of childbearing and, anyway, Sarah has been barren. The child is born exactly when God said and is a boy, as he said. God has been true to his promise.

No wonder Sarah now laughs with joy and wonderment (21:6–7). The child is named Isaac, which means 'he laughs', suggesting that Abraham also saw the funny side. We are invited to chuckle with them as well: 'everyone who hears about this will laugh with me' (v. 6), says Sarah. Such is the effect of grace in all our lives. It brings a lightness of heart, a deep sense of gratitude, an awareness that we are blessed. Grace humbles us, draws us to worship and thanksgiving and moves us to be kind towards others.

Prayer

Lord, your outrageous grace still amazes me!

TONY HORSFALL

GENESIS 22:1–2, 13–14 (NIV)

The provider

Some time later God tested Abraham. He said to him, 'Abraham!' 'Here I am,' he replied. Then God said, 'Take your son, your only son, Isaac, whom you love, and go to the region of Moriah. Sacrifice him there as a burnt offering on a mountain I will tell you about.'... Abraham looked up and there in a thicket he saw a ram caught by its horns. He went over and took the ram and sacrificed it as a burnt offering instead of his son. So Abraham called that place The Lord Will Provide. And to this day it is said, 'On the mountain of the Lord it will be provided.'

There can have been few tests of faith as challenging as the one Abraham experiences on Mount Moriah. His faith is stretched to the absolute limit as he is asked to sacrifice his son and, with him, the covenant promises of future blessing. Yet, somehow, Abraham finds it in his heart to obey, even though every step up the mountainside must have felt like torture.

The writer to the Hebrews provides us with an insight into Abraham's thinking at this time: 'Abraham reasoned that God could raise the dead, and figuratively speaking, he did receive Isaac back from death' (11:19). As he considered God's character and what he knew of his faithfulness and love, it was inconceivable to him that this would be the end. It must mean that God would bring him back to life.

To modern ears, this whole story is problematical and we wonder how God could require such a sacrifice. 'Would he ask it of me?' we might nervously ask. God, however, never asks us to go beyond the level of our faith or do anything without supplying us with the grace to do it.

Abraham was not required to go the whole way in offering his son, for it was his willingness that God was seeking. All along, an alternative had been in waiting—a ram caught in a nearby bush. God is the one who provides, even in our moments of extreme need, and at just the right time.

Prayer

Lord, you are my provider.

TONY HORSFALL

GENESIS 24:1–4 (NIV)

God of heaven and earth

Abraham was now old and well advanced in years, and the Lord had blessed him in every way. He said to the chief servant in his household, the one in charge of all that he had, 'Put your hand under my thigh. I want you to swear by the Lord, the God of heaven and the God of earth, that you will not get a wife for my son from the daughters of the Canaanites, among whom I am living, but will go to my country and my own relatives and get a wife for my son Isaac.'

By now Abraham is 137 years old. Sarah has just died, aged 127, and, no doubt, Abraham is facing up to his own mortality. The purchase of a burial ground from Ephron the Hittite (23:17–20) would have been a sobering reminder that the day would come when he, too, would be 'gathered to his people' (25:8).

Such moments of awareness can be spiritually significant. Abraham pauses to look back over a long and varied life, with satisfaction. As he ponders his memories, it is with a deep sense of God's goodness, for 'the Lord had blessed him in every way' (24:1). The backward glance can indeed make our hearts glad and strengthen our faith as we see how God has guided and guarded us.

Such moments can also cause us to consider the future and make plans for what is yet to be. For Abraham, this means finding a suitable wife for his son Isaac, through whom the promises of God will be worked out. His servant is despatched to Abraham's native land to search for a girl from the same clan. Providentially, he is led to Rebekah —another example of the kindness and faithfulness of God (24:27) and exactly the right choice (v. 67).

Abraham knew the God of heaven and earth, the one who guides us on our earthly pilgrimage and brings us safely home to heaven itself. Nowhere is outside of his control and his purposes are being worked out in all the events of our lives. Our lives are safe in his hands.

Prayer

Lord, guide my steps today; be at work in all that happens.

TONY HORSFALL

HEBREWS 11:8–10 (NIV)

Architect and builder

> By faith Abraham, when called to go to a place he would later receive as his inheritance, obeyed and went, even though he did not know where he was going. By faith he made his home in the promised land like a stranger in a foreign country; he lived in tents, as did Isaac and Jacob, who were heirs with him of the same promise. For he was looking forward to the city with foundations, whose architect and builder is God.

As we come to the final reading in the story of Abraham, we turn to this summary of his life to see the bigger picture. We are reminded that he was brought up in the city of Ur—one of the wonders of the ancient world, but also full of idolatry.

Looking at the fine buildings around him and the mighty ziggurat that dominated the skyline, Abraham was forced to ponder the meaning of life and face the emptiness within his own soul. He longed for something deeper and more substantial than Sumerian deities could offer. He found it in the living God, the God of glory who appeared to him and shone the light of life into his darkened heart.

From that moment, Abraham had glimpsed something more real and lasting, something eternal. He began to look forward to a city with lasting foundations that would never be covered by the sands of time. He saw that God was building a heavenly city, according to his own design, and he wanted to be part of it.

This vision dominated his life and caused him to leave behind the city of Ur, becoming a pilgrim. It affected how he lived, for he believed that here on earth there could be no permanent dwelling place. Together with his family, he chose not to become too settled or at home here, keeping his eye all the time on another, better country—heaven itself.

It is a perspective on life that we believers today might well reflect on, for we are so easily immersed in the materialism of our times, forgetting that the world we see is not our final home.

Prayer

Lord, let me grasp eternal values.

TONY HORSFALL

God and the Olympics

'The Games of the XXX Olympiad in 2012 are awarded to the city of London.' Those words spoken by Jacques Rogge, president of the International Olympic Committee, on 6 July 2005 were life-changing for many people. Now the Games are upon us. The new facilities are ready. The East End of London has been transformed. The tickets have been sold. For most of us, the Olympics will never again be held in the UK in our lifetimes.

Many of us are proud that the focus of the world is on London. Others, to be honest, are irritated that the Games will dominate the media or concerned about the cost to the taxpayer. Some will have tickets or will be part of the event as official volunteers. Others may be disappointed to have missed out on tickets to the event they really wanted to see.

'OK,' you may be thinking, 'that is all very interesting, but I thought I was about to do my daily Bible reading rather than worry about the impact of the Olympics or how many medals my country might win.' We have probably all heard the joke about tennis in the Bible—Joseph served in Pharaoh's courts—or that the football team Solomon supported was Queen of the South (1 Kings 10), but has the Bible really anything to say about sport?

The God of the Bible reveals himself as interested in all human activity, including sport. God is to be worshipped not just on Sunday morning but all week, 24/7. If we are involved in sport—as a player, coach, spectator or even parent of a participant—we should remember that we are representatives of Jesus Christ. Should our relationship with God not be as relevant when we are playing or watching sport as when we are in church?

As you reflect on the Olympics from a biblical perspective, I pray that you will see them as an opportunity to be thankful, to worship, to serve and to share the good news. For more information on the Olympics, see www.london2012.com and note, too, that more than 30 different resources have been produced to help Christians share their faith with friends (see the More Than Gold website at: www.morethangoldresources.org.uk).

J. Stuart Weir

GENESIS 1:1–5 (NIV)

Did God create sport?

> In the beginning God created the heavens and the earth. Now the earth was formless and empty, darkness was over the surface of the deep, and the Spirit of God was hovering over the waters. And God said, 'Let there be light,' and there was light. God saw that the light was good, and he separated the light from the darkness. God called the light 'day', and the darkness he called 'night'. And there was evening, and there was morning—the first day.

As most people know, Genesis is the first book of the Bible and contains in the first two chapters a magnificent account of the creation of the world. God is the creator of every single thing in this world, which—the story pronounces over and over again—'was good'. At the end of Genesis 1, we read, 'God saw all that he had made and it was very good' (v. 31).

This writing is meant to evoke praise and awe. If we understand this and remember it as we read, our attitude to God will be transformed. We will realise that we must worship him in all things and at all times.

So, did God actually create sport as well as everything else? The answer is yes and no. Of course God did not create sport—people did. It was not God who first kicked a football; it was a person. God did not create the games we play, but God did create people and made them able to run, jump, kick and catch. Sport is simply organised play, in which we have the opportunity to use the talents that God has given us.

It is true that the world of sport can be a very godless place but, sadly, it is undeniably true that all aspects of life can be godless. As an activity in which we can use the gifts and abilities that God has given us, sport is as valuable and significant as any other part of our lives. Playing sport is as legitimate as any other human activity.

Reflection

If I really believed that my involvement in sport was an integral part of my Christian life, how would it change my attitude to sport?

J. STUART WEIR

GENESIS 1:27–28 (NIV)

Where is your identity?

So God created human beings in his own image, in the image of God he created them; male and female he created them. God blessed them and said to them, 'Be fruitful and increase in number; fill the earth and subdue it. Rule over the fish in the sea and the birds in the sky and over every living creature that moves on the ground.'

Sport has a performance-based identity. You are judged by what you have achieved—'He's an Olympian', 'She has won Olympic gold', 'He broke the world record', 'She is ranked number 3 in the world' and so on. Have you ever noticed how sportspeople introduce themselves—'I am a footballer', 'I am a runner', 'I am a cyclist'? When two runners meet, they relate to each other—they talk distance, races, training, shoes and related technical stuff.

We, too, can identify ourselves as runners or cyclists, but, deeper than that, we are followers of Jesus. It is that relationship which defines us and gives us our value and significance as people. Jesus wants us to be involved in the world of sport, but also to remember that we are there to represent him.

We are called into a relationship with Jesus. We are not asked to sign up for a cause. That is the essence of our being Christians: to be in a relationship with him. This is our number one priority and everything else is to be secondary. That relationship with Jesus has an ultimate purpose—to share the good news with others.

Have you ever wondered why the Ten Commandments were so strict about forbidding the people to create any images of God (Exodus 20:4)? It is simply because Genesis 1:26 has taught us that there is already an image of God in the world—you and me.

I love the way the former Leeds United football club chaplain, John Jackson, put it: 'I don't go into the football club to take Jesus. He is already there. I just go in case he needs an errand boy.'

Reflection

I am made in the image of God. I am his representative in the sports club, at work, everywhere.

J. STUART WEIR

1 CORINTHIANS 9:24–27 (NIV)

The Christian as an athlete

Do you not know that in a race all the runners run, but only one gets the prize? Run in such a way as to get the prize. Everyone who competes in the games goes into strict training. They do it to get a crown that will not last; but we do it to get a crown that will last for ever. Therefore I do not run like someone running aimlessly; I do not fight like a boxer beating the air. No, I strike a blow to my body and make it my slave so that after I have preached to others, I myself will not be disqualified for the prize.

As I sat in the media seats in Beijing watching Usain Bolt smash the world record in the 100 metres, I confess that I was so taken up with his achievement that I did not give a thought to the other seven runners in the final or the 72 who had been eliminated in the heats—or the thousands who had not made the Olympics. It was all about the one who got the prize.

Paul is not trying to write a theology of sport here—any more than he is writing a theology of war or of agriculture when he tells Timothy to be a soldier of Jesus Christ and to be like a farmer (2 Timothy 2:3–7).

Just as the athlete has to be focused, disciplined, single-minded, so should the Christian. Former world heavyweight boxing champion Muhammad Ali used to say, 'The fight is won or lost far away from the witnesses—behind the lines, in the gym and out on the road, long before I dance under those lights.' Similarly, it is the time we spend alone with God—away from witnesses, alone in the early morning, perhaps—that will prepare us for public acts of service.

The kudos of being Olympic champion, for most people, lasts only four years until a new champion comes along. The Christian's crown will last forever. That should be a real motivation to us.

Prayer

Lord, as I watch great Olympians, help me to be as committed to spiritual disciplines as they are to their training.

J. STUART WEIR

ROMANS 12:1–2 (NIV)

Worshipping God in sport

Therefore, I urge you, brothers and sisters, in view of God's mercy, to offer your bodies as a living sacrifice, holy and pleasing to God—this is your true and proper worship. Do not conform to the pattern of this world, but be transformed by the renewing of your mind. Then you will be able to test and approve what God's will is—his good, pleasing and perfect will.

As 'living sacrifices' (v. 1)! When Paul writes about living sacrifices, that is an oxymoron. Sacrifices are not alive. You chop their heads off, or stick a stake in them. Paul, on purpose, uses a seemingly ridiculous phrase.

Now if you are a sportsperson, the idea of offering your body as a living sacrifice has extra meaning. Having a body is essential if you are going to play, but we are asked to offer that body as a living sacrifice, a sacrifice that wriggles on the altar. This means we must live as people who have given our bodies to Jesus Christ.

Paul calls it 'your true and proper worship' (v. 1). Another translation phrases this as your 'spiritual act of worship'. Now let us clear from our minds any idea that worship is restricted to singing songs or that worship is an hour on a Sunday. We are called to give our bodies to God to please him, as an act of worship, a full-time lifestyle activity. That is what worship is—giving every piece of your mind, body, time, everything to God.

The words 'do not conform' (v. 2) are ones that we need to hear again and again. They must always be a great part of the content of Christian exhortation. As Christians, we have always to confess that, to a painfully large extent, our lives are conformed to the values of this age.

Paul also says 'be transformed' (v. 2). This transformation is not the Christian's own doing, but the work of the Holy Spirit. We have a responsibility, however, to let ourselves be transformed, to respond to the leading of God's Spirit. We are to live differently in the world as a result.

Reflection

What are the situations in sport or in life where it is hardest not to conform to the standards of the world?

J. STUART WEIR

ROMANS 12:12–18 (NIV)

Christian sports ethic

> Be joyful in hope, patient in affliction, faithful in prayer. Share with the Lord's people who are in need. Practise hospitality. Bless those who persecute you; bless and do not curse. Rejoice with those who rejoice; mourn with those who mourn. Live in harmony with one another. Do not be proud, but be willing to associate with people of low position. Do not be conceited. Do not repay anyone evil for evil. Be careful to do what is right in the eyes of everyone. If it is possible, as far as it depends on you, live at peace with everyone.

In Romans 1—8, Paul gives, arguably, the best summary of the gospel in the whole Bible. Then, in chapters 9—11, he deals with the issues of the ongoing status of God's people, Israel, before getting practical in chapter 12. As we saw yesterday, he starts the chapter, 'Therefore, I urge you… in view of God's mercy to…' God's grace is wonderful, but it has implications for how we live.

This passage is not just practical, it is *intensely* practical. What is the mark of a Christian? That they go to church every Sunday and attend a house group mid-week? No—the mark of the Christian is to be patient, joyful, faithful, not proud, peaceful, prayerful, living in harmony with one another. If it were a choice, I would prefer to commit simply to going to church and house group.

This passage has so much to say that is relevant to sport—and to life. There is so much pride in sport (and in life). Paul says, 'Do not be proud' (v. 16), having already said, 'Do not think of yourself more highly than you ought' (v. 3). In the performance-driven environment of sport, it is easy to take pride in your ability and achievements, but Christ calls us to be humble. In a competitive, 'me-first' world, we are to be peacemakers, people who live in harmony with others. We are to be those who defuse conflicts rather than those who cause them.

Prayer

Thank you, Lord, for all your people who are involved in the Olympics
as athletes, coaches, officials or volunteers.
Help them to be humble peacemakers.

J. STUART WEIR

MATTHEW 22:35–40 (NIV)

Loving your neighbour

One of them, an expert in the law, tested [Jesus] with this question: 'Teacher, which is the greatest commandment in the Law?' Jesus replied: '"Love the Lord your God with all your heart and with all your soul and with all your mind." This is the first and greatest commandment. And the second is like it: "Love your neighbour as yourself." All the Law and the Prophets hang on these two commandments.'

'I don't go out there to love my enemy, I go out there to squash him,' said Jimmy Connors, the American tennis player. Competition is part of sport; we need competition in order to judge our own performance. The literal meaning of 'compete' is to strive together. Two things confuse us when we consider Jesus' summary of godly love as it relates to the issue of loving our opponents on the sportsfield—our understanding of 'love' and our mental picture of 'opponent'. So much coaching in sport involves seeing the opponent as the enemy. You are not thought to be competitive unless you are mentally swearing at the opposition.

Wait a minute—we need opponents. If you were marooned alone on a desert island—an island with a state-of-the-art tennis court—it would be very frustrating. What is the point of a tennis court, balls and a racquet if there is no one to compete against?

People often think of love as soft—meaning that we cannot be loving *and* competitive. I once interviewed the Juventus and Italy defender Nicola Legrottaglie and asked him about this tension. He replied, 'So you think that because I am a Christian I should just let my opponent score?' He had no problem being a Christian and being competitive.

There is no doubt that humility, meekness and gentleness are essential parts of the Christian character, but we still have to work out how this affects our attitude to competitive sport. We are to act with meekness and gentleness in our relationships with others without losing our competitive edge. No one said it was going to be easy.

Reflection

If you cannot play sport in a spirit of loving your neighbour, then, as a Christian, you cannot play at all.

J. STUART WEIR

ACTS 1:7–9 (NIV)

Reaching the world of sport for Christ

> [Jesus] said to them: 'It is not for you to know the times or dates the Father has set by his own authority. But you will receive power when the Holy Spirit comes on you; and you will be my witnesses in Jerusalem, and in all Judea and Samaria, and to the ends of the earth.' After he said this, he was taken up before their very eyes and a cloud hid him from their sight.

Statistics show that a high proportion of people who become Christians do so partly as a result of a friendship with another Christian. There are few better ways to make and develop friendships than sport.

We are all called to be witnesses where God has placed us. Sportspeople have the opportunity to demonstrate the image of God in an environment that is often lacking in the knowledge of God. Christians have found opportunities to share the gospel in gyms and on golf courses, tennis courts and sports fields the world over. Spiritual seekers may not come to church, but, by seeing the sports club as your missionfield, you can take Christ to them.

If God has given you a love for sport, never feel guilty about spending time at your club. Just be intentional about praying for people and seeking to share the good news of Jesus with them.

People enjoy watching sport with others as the atmosphere is better than at home. You could choose an Olympic event next week and invite friends to watch it with you somewhere. A big football or rugby international in the autumn will work equally well. You could even show the game on a big screen at church. Think of two or three friends with whom you share an interest in sport. Pray for them and an opportunity to share Jesus with them.

If sport is not your passion, be patient. The Olympics will soon be over! Try to recognise the joy they give to many and the opportunities they give to build bridges in the community.

Prayer

Thank you, Lord, for our bodies, which enable us to do sport—or just go for a walk in your beautiful creation. Help us to enjoy your gift of sport, but also to see its potential to reach out to others.

J. STUART WEIR

2 Kings 1—4

The events of the chapters we will be looking at over the next couple of weeks take place in a time of huge political and religious turmoil. Israel's existence as a united nation had come to an explosive end after the death of David's son Solomon, and the resulting two kingdoms of Israel and Judah existed uneasily alongside one another. During the times of Elijah and Elisha, both kingdoms clashed repeatedly with the Syrians (Aramaeans) of Damascus and Israel lost control of Moab (2 Kings 1:1; 3:4–27).

In an age when politics and religion were inseparably joined, the instability in religious beliefs and experience was no less unsettling. David had captured Jerusalem from the Jebusites (2 Samuel 5:6–10), making it the strategic centre of his kingdom, and his installing of the ark of the covenant there also made it the kingdom's religious and spiritual centre (6:1–19). When Solomon succeeded David all seemed set fair: the kingdom had economic and military security and all were united in their commitment to the God of Israel (23:1–7). By the end of his reign, however, Solomon had reneged on his religious allegiance and the biblical account points to this betrayal as the reason for the splitting of the kingdom (1 Kings 11:1–13).

The period covered by the prophetic reigns of Elijah and Elisha was approximately 870–790BC and we pick up the story as the life and work of Elijah comes to its close and his prophetic mantle is passed on—literally—to Elisha. As the events of these chapters unfold, we may find ourselves both attracted to and alienated by the material they contain. Attracted, because we will witness instances of loving compassion and caring response to human need (2 Kings 4:1–7); alienated, because the actions attributed to God can sometimes seem cruel and excessive (2:23–25). We need, if possible, to resist the temptation to judge the interpretations of an earlier age by the understanding of our own. What we are given, which holds true for all ages, is a picture of divine concern for the 'big picture' in the sweep of history across all ages and times. That same divine involvement is also seen in the intimate and personal; and it prepares the way for the New Testament understanding of a God for whom 'even the hairs of your head are all counted' (Matthew 10:30).

Barbara Mosse

2 KINGS 1:1–4 (NRSV)

Is there no God in Israel?

> After the death of Ahab, Moab rebelled against Israel. Ahaziah had fallen through the lattice in his upper chamber in Samaria, and lay injured; so he sent messengers, telling them, 'Go, inquire of Baal-zebub, the god of Ekron, whether I shall recover from this injury.' But the angel of the Lord said to Elijah the Tishbite, 'Get up, go to meet the messengers of the king of Samaria, and say to them, "Is it because there is no God in Israel that you are going to inquire of Baal-zebub, the god of Ekron?" Now therefore, thus says the Lord, "You shall not leave the bed to which you have gone, but you shall surely die."' So Elijah went.

After an abrupt reference to the rebellion of Moab against Israel after the death of King Ahab, 2 Kings begins with the plight of Ahaziah—one of many Israelite kings who 'did what was evil in the sight of the Lord' (1 Kings 22:52). He has been mortally injured in a fall and sends messengers to inquire of Baal-zebub, the god of Ekron, about his chances of recovery. An angel sends Elijah to intercept the messengers and challenge the intention of their lord: 'Is it because there is no God in Israel that you are going to inquire of Baal-zebub?' (v. 3). Without waiting for their reply, Elijah will pronounce Ahaziah's fate: 'You shall not leave the bed to which you have gone, but you shall surely die' (v. 4). In a battle of divinities, this is an unequal contest and Ahaziah is putting his trust in a god who has no power or influence.

When events spiral out of our control, where do we put our trust? To whom or what do we reach out? Practical help from others may well be part of God's response to our need, but can only take us so far. Ultimately, the challenge is to 'go out into the darkness, and put your hand into the hand of God' (Minnie Louise Haskins, 1908).

Prayer

'I trust in you, O Lord; I say, "You are my God." My times are in your hand… save me in your steadfast love' (Psalm 31:14–16).

BARBARA MOSSE

2 KINGS 1:9–17 (NRSV, ABRIDGED)

Fire from heaven

Then the king sent to [Elijah] a captain of fifty with his fifty men. He went up to Elijah, who was sitting on the top of a hill, and said to him, 'O man of God, the king says, "Come down."' But Elijah answered the captain of fifty, 'If I am a man of God, let fire come down from heaven...' Then fire came down from heaven, and consumed him and his fifty. Again the king sent to him another captain of fifty with his fifty... Again the king sent the captain of a third fifty... [He] fell on his knees before Elijah and entreated him, 'O man of God, please let my life, and the life of these fifty servants of yours, be precious in your sight.'... Then the angel of the Lord said to Elijah, 'Go down with him; do not be afraid of him.'... [Ahaziah] died according to the word of the Lord that Elijah had spoken.

If Ahaziah's peremptory command and display of military strength are intended to intimidate Elijah, they fail completely, as the prophet calls down fire from heaven to consume the first two captains and their men. Fear emboldens the third captain to speak for himself. He acknowledges the power of God, then begs Elijah to be merciful and spare his life (v. 14). Reassured by an angel, Elijah goes down with the captain and delivers his message to Ahaziah in person. (vv. 16).

We may stumble over yet another example of the innocent being slaughtered, apparently at God's command, but Elijah's world is not our world and the norms by which it operated are different from our own. If we are able to get behind the cultural accretions and religious perceptions of an earlier age, we will find an eternal truth. We will discover that the God whom we worship cannot be commanded or summoned to fulfil our desires when we otherwise ignore him. Our journey, like that of the Israelites before us, is a slow and sometimes painful process of learning to 'strive first for the kingdom of God' (Matthew 6:33).

Prayer

'Create in me a clean heart, O God,
and put a new and right spirit within me' (Psalm 51:10).

BARBARA MOSSE

2 Kings 2:1–2, 6–8 (NRSV, abridged)

'As the Lord lives... I will not leave you'

> Now when the Lord was about to take Elijah up to heaven by a whirlwind, Elijah and Elisha were on their way from Gilgal. Elijah said to Elisha, 'Stay here; for the Lord has sent me as far as Bethel.' But Elisha said, 'As the Lord lives, and as you yourself live, I will not leave you.'... Then Elijah said to him, 'Stay here; for the Lord has sent me to the Jordan.' But he said, 'As the Lord lives, and as you yourself live, I will not leave you.' So the two of them went on. Fifty men of the company of prophets also went, and stood at some distance from them, as they both were standing by the Jordan. Then Elijah took his mantle, rolled it up and struck the water; the water was parted to one side and to the other, until the two of them crossed on dry ground.

What we know of Elisha's background is sketchy and comes from just a few verses in 1 Kings 19:16–21. He was the son of Shaphat and was working as a ploughman prior to his meeting with Elijah, who marked him as his successor by throwing his mantle over him (v. 19). Bidding farewell to his family and disposing of the tools of his trade, Elisha followed Elijah and became his servant (v. 21).

Today's episode crackles with tension and foreboding. Elijah's departure is imminent and he appears to be trying to spare Elisha the sight of his final passing. Three times Elijah urges Elisha to stop while he travels on alone, but each time Elisha affirms his determination to go with him. Elisha's unhappiness and unease, however, are tangible and he urges the prophets, who remind him of Elijah's imminent departure, to be silent (2 Kings 2:3, 5).

On arriving at the Jordan, Elijah strikes the water with his rolled-up mantle; the waters part, and the two men cross. The prophet's actions here are deeply significant, and are reminiscent of Moses' parting of the water of the Sea of Reeds (Exodus 14:21–22). The implication is that Elijah is a prophet carrying the same divine authority as Moses.

Reflection

Consider prayerfully the difficulty in letting go of a known past, in order that the unknown future may take shape.

Barbara Mosse

2 KINGS 2:9–12 (NRSV)

Chariots of fire

When they had crossed [the Jordan], Elijah said to Elisha, 'Tell me what I may do for you, before I am taken from you.' Elisha said, 'Please let me inherit a double share of your spirit.' He responded, 'You have asked a hard thing; yet, if you see me as I am being taken from you, it will be granted you; if not, it will not.' As they continued walking and talking, a chariot of fire and horses of fire separated the two of them, and Elijah ascended in a whirlwind to heaven. Elisha kept watching and crying out, 'Father, father! The chariots of Israel and its horsemen!' But when he could no longer see him, he grasped his own clothes and tore them in two pieces.

Our passage for today falls into two parts: first, there is Elisha's request that he might inherit a double share of his master's spirit, which is followed by the departure of Elijah 'in a whirlwind' to heaven (v. 11). The two sections are linked by the phrase, 'As they continued walking and talking...' (v. 11). The extraordinary request and the events that followed are enclosing activities of routine normality.

The prophet and his disciple have crossed the Jordan river and Elijah now asks Elisha if there is anything further he can do for him. Elisha's request for 'a double share' of Elijah's spirit' (v. 9) is consistent with the legal right of the firstborn to inherit two-thirds of his father's inheritance (Deuteronomy 21:15–17). Despite the fact that Elisha has been set apart by God as Elijah's successor, Elijah tells Elisha he has asked 'a hard thing' that was not his to grant (v. 10). The sign that the request had been granted would be for Elisha to see his master taken into heaven.

Transition times in our lives are never easy and, for both Elijah and Elisha, these dramatic events confronted them with the need to let go of the securities of the past and trust to God's enabling for the unknown future.

Prayer

Lord, let not the past be so dear to me that I limit the future. Amen

Source unknown

BARBARA MOSSE

2 Kings 2:13–18 (NRSV, abridged)

The spirit of Elijah

> [Elisha] picked up the mantle of Elijah that had fallen from him, and went back and stood on the bank of the Jordan. He took the mantle... and struck the water, saying, 'Where is the Lord, the God of Elijah?' When he had struck the water, the water was parted to the one side and to the other, and Elisha went over. When the company of prophets who were at Jericho saw him at a distance, they declared, 'The spirit of Elijah rests on Elisha.' They came to meet him and... said to him, 'See now, we have fifty strong men... please let them go and seek your master... He responded, 'No, do not send them.' But when they urged him until he was ashamed, he said, 'Send them.' So they sent fifty men who searched for three days but did not find him... [Elisha] said to them, 'Did I not say to you, Do not go?'

Elisha's grief is heart-rending and these few verses are full of the pain and anguish of his loss. His cry—'Where is the Lord, the God of Elijah?'—as he strikes the water seems to embody a seething mixture of deep grief, anger, defiance and desolation.

Elisha's desire that he should inherit Elijah's spiritual legacy is immediately confirmed as the waters part. The watching company of prophets are also convinced, giving him the honour and respect they previously gave to Elijah (v. 15).

Then, curiously, the prophets urge Elisha to let them search for Elijah in the surrounding countryside, because 'it may be that the Lord has caught him up and thrown him down on some mountain or into some valley' (v. 16). It is possible that this fruitless search for Elijah illustrates something of the difficulty Elisha and the prophets were having in accepting Elijah's passing; a difficulty that may have been aggravated because there was no body to bury. The search made it possible for them finally to accept Elijah's passing and enabled them to move on.

Reflection

'When you pass through the waters, I will be with you;
and through the rivers, they shall not overwhelm you...
For I am the Lord your God' (Isaiah 43:2–3).

Barbara Mosse

2 KINGS 2:19–24 (NRSV, ABRIDGED)

Blessing and curse

Now the people of the city said to Elisha, 'The location of this city is good, as my lord sees; but the water is bad, and the land is unfruitful.' He said, 'Bring me a new bowl, and put salt in it.' So they brought it to him. Then he went to the spring of water and threw the salt into it... The water has been wholesome to this day... He went up from there to Bethel; and... some small boys came out of the city and jeered at him, saying, 'Go away, baldhead!...' When he turned round and saw them, he cursed them in the name of the Lord. Then two she-bears came out of the woods and mauled forty-two of the boys.

Elisha's ministry begins in earnest with two intriguing episodes. He first purifies Jericho's poisoned water system by throwing salt into it—an incident that offers sympathetic resonances with Moses' sweetening of the bitter water at Marah by throwing wood into it (Exodus 15:23–25). This life-bringing miracle is immediately followed, however, by a disturbing event with no comfortable explanation. Elisha curses 'in the name of the Lord' (2 Kings 2:24) a group of small boys (v. 23, NRSV) or youths (NIV), who repeatedly taunt him with the nickname 'baldhead'. This may have passed as simply a knee-jerk response were it not for the subsequent mauling of a number of the boys or youths by two bears. An implied link between the curse and the bear-mauling makes Elisha's actions (and, consequently, God's) seem vindictive, petty and morally indefensible.

There may be a deeper explanation, however. The NIV records the taunt as 'Go on up, you baldhead!'—possibly a scurrilous reference to Elijah's being 'taken up' into heaven. If so, an apparently harmless episode of name-calling takes on another meaning. The boys are, in effect, wishing Elijah dead and treating the holy God of Israel with derision. That said, no interpretation is problem-free.

Reflection

'I call heaven and earth to witness against you today that I have set before you life and death, blessings and curses. Choose life so that you and your descendants may live, loving the Lord your God' (Deuteronomy 30:19–20).

BARBARA MOSSE

2 KINGS 3:9–12, 15–20 (NRSV, ABRIDGED)

Water in the desert

[The three kings] set out; and when they had made a roundabout march of seven days, there was no water for the army or for the animals that were with them... Jehoshaphat said, 'Is there no prophet of the Lord here, through whom we may inquire of the Lord?' Then one of the servants of the king of Israel answered, 'Elisha... who used to pour water on the hands of Elijah, is here.' Jehoshaphat said, 'The word of the Lord is with him.'... [Elisha said] '... Get me a musician.'... And he said, 'Thus says the Lord, "I will make this wadi full of pools."... He will also hand Moab over to you.'... The next day... suddenly water began to flow from the direction of Edom, until the country was filled with water.

The first eight verses of this chapter pick up on events alluded to in 1:1—the rebellion of the Moabites and the campaign against them by the kings of Israel, Judah and Edom. When the royal trio and their armies find themselves without water, it is striking that Jehoshaphat urges they seek the guidance of the Lord, in stark contrast to Ahaziah's earlier seeking of the wisdom of Baal (1:2).

Jehoshaphat knows that Elisha is a man of God, but Elisha has been unimpressed with the apostasy of Jehoram and his parents (3:13) and makes no attempt to hide his impatience. Jehoshaphat, however, did 'what was right in the sight of the Lord' (1 Kings 22:43) and Elisha held him in high regard. On this basis, he agrees to act and makes it clear that, without Jehoshaphat, the others would receive 'neither a look nor a glance' (2 Kings 3:14). It is interesting that Elisha then calls for music (v. 15), which seems to have functioned much as did David's playing for Saul (1 Samuel 16:23), calming his agitation and enabling the power of the Lord to work.

The prophecy is fulfilled: the land fills with water and there is a further promise of victory over the Moabites.

Reflection

In the turmoil of life, with its patterning of light and shadow, ensure that you sit in the silent presence of God, seeking his still, small voice in the depths of your heart.

BARBARA MOSSE

2 Kings 3:21–27 (NRSV, abridged)

Evil triumphant?

When all the Moabites heard that the kings had come up to fight against them, all who were able to put on armour... were called out and were drawn up at the frontier. When they rose early in the morning, and the sun shone upon the water, the Moabites saw the water opposite them as red as blood. They said, 'This is blood; the kings must have fought together, and killed one another. Now then, Moab, to the spoil!' But when they came to the camp of Israel, the Israelites rose up and attacked the Moabites, who fled before them... When the king of Moab saw that the battle was going against him... he took his firstborn son... and offered him as a burnt-offering on the wall. And great wrath came upon Israel, so they withdrew from him and returned to their own land.

The narrative continues with a graphic picture of the Moabites, armed and waiting for the enemy. Mistakenly assuming the enemy kings have been fighting among themselves, they descend on the Israelite camp. The Moabites flee as the Israelites attack, chasing them through the land in an orgy of destruction. In a fit of desperation, the Moabite king sacrifices his firstborn son and heir on the city walls as a burnt-offering to his god (a practice that was anathema to the Israelites; see Deuteronomy 12:31).

Here, however, the narrative takes a totally unexpected twist. With victory in their grasp, 'great wrath came upon Israel' and they simply stopped fighting and returned home (v. 27). Nobody seems really sure whose 'wrath' is being referred to here. The NIV opts for the Moabites, with 'The fury against Israel was great' (v. 27), while others assume it is the wrath of God. On this interpretation, the salvation and blessing of God are instantly turned against the Israelites in response to their excessive destructiveness (Deuteronomy 20:19–20). The problem here is that, far from going beyond their remit, the Israelites appear to have obeyed the instructions given them through Elisha's prophecy to the letter (3:18–19). Perhaps the writer was as baffled as we are.

Prayer

Take us, Lord, we pray, in all our confusion and complexity, and make of our lives a tapestry of beauty to your glory.

Barbara Mosse

2 Kings 4:1–7 (NRSV, abridged)

The widow's oil

> Now the wife of a member of the company of prophets cried to Elisha, 'Your servant my husband is dead; and... a creditor has come to take my two children as slaves.' Elisha said to her, 'What shall I do for you?... She answered, 'Your servant has nothing in the house, except a jar of oil.' He said, 'Go outside, borrow vessels from all your neighbours, empty vessels and not just a few. Then go in... and start pouring into all these vessels...' She kept pouring... [and] said to her son, 'Bring me another vessel.' But he said to her, 'There are no more.' Then the oil stopped flowing. She came and told the man of God, and he said, 'Go, sell the oil and pay your debts, and you and your children can live on the rest.'

From the wide, theatrical canvas of political intrigues and battles, the focus now moves to a group of intimate and domestic miraculous incidents.

The first of these involves Elisha's rescue of the family of a fellow prophet who has died. His widow was liable for his unpaid debts and, unable to pay, she faces seeing her children sold into slavery to redeem the debt (Nehemiah 5:3–5). Elisha has no authority to prevent this catastrophe, but his miraculous increasing of the small amount of oil she possessed not only redeems her debts, but also provides enough for the family to live on. The miracle provides a close parallel to the one performed by Elijah for the widow of Zarephath, who was in a situation of comparable domestic crisis (1 Kings 17:8–16).

Sometimes it is not clear how we should act in a given situation. When this happens, our only way forward may lie in a silent waiting on God. In the silence, an alternative approach, previously hidden, may begin to emerge from the confusion.

Reflection

'Teacher, this woman was caught in the very act of committing adultery. Now in the law Moses commanded us to stone such women. Now what do you say?'... Jesus bent down and wrote with his finger on the ground... 'Let anyone among you who is without sin be the first to throw a stone at her' (John 8:4–7).

Barbara Mosse

2 KINGS 4:8–10 (NRSV)

A place of refreshment

One day Elisha was passing through Shunem, where a wealthy woman lived, who urged him to have a meal. So whenever he passed that way, he would stop there for a meal. She said to her husband, 'Look, I am sure that this man who regularly passes our way is a holy man of God. Let us make a small roof chamber with walls, and put there for him a bed, a table, a chair, and a lamp, so that he can stay there whenever he comes to us.'

However effective his public ministry may have been, Elisha would soon have been 'running on empty' if it had not been for this kind of quiet, unsung ministry of hospitality. A necessity for survival among the nomadic desert peoples, the practice of hospitality was also a matter of sacred honour—biblical examples abound (see, for example, Genesis 18:1–8; 24:28–32). The practice continued in New Testament times and Jesus benefited greatly from the loving welcome offered him in the home of Mary, Martha and Lazarus at Bethany (Luke 10:38). The disciples on the Emmaus road urged the stranger who accompanied them to stay the night before continuing his journey (Luke 24:29) and Jesus himself reserved some of his highest praise for those who offered hospitality (Matthew 25:35).

It seems that the Shunammite woman does not initially know the status or identity of her guest, but, as she begins to get to know him, his calling as a holy man becomes clear. She is a rich woman (2 Kings 4:8) and, in addition to offering meals, her wealth enables her and her husband to extend their house in order to provide Elisha with a furnished bedroom of his own.

There is a persistent challenge that threads its way through all the biblical references to hospitality. Whatever the situation, there is a lavishness, an open-hearted generosity that seeks to spend itself, even if it puts the host's household in some difficulty or danger (Genesis 19:8). The instinct appears to be to provide as warmly and generously as you can—and only then, if necessary, ask questions.

Reflection

How openhearted and generous is our own hospitality?

BARBARA MOSSE

2 KINGS 4:11–17 (NRSV, ABRIDGED)

The child of promise

One day when [Elisha] came there, he went up to the chamber and laid down there. He said to his servant Gehazi, 'Call the Shunammite woman.' When he had called her, she stood before him. He said to him, 'Say to her, Since you have taken all this trouble for us, what may be done for you? Would you have a word spoken on your behalf to the king or to the commander of the army?' She answered, 'I live among my own people.' He said, 'What then may be done for her?' Gehazi answered, 'Well, she has no son, and her husband is old.' He said, 'Call her.'... He said [to her], 'At this season, in due time, you shall embrace a son.' She replied, 'No, my Lord, O man of God; do not deceive your servant.' The woman conceived and bore a son at that season, in due time, as Elisha had declared to her.

It is clear that the woman's aim in extending hospitality to Elisha was purely altruistic, as, when she is asked what can be done for her, she replies that she has everything she needs (v. 13). Gehazi spots the one thing lacking: 'She has no son, and her husband is old' (v. 14). So, as the Shunammite woman stands at the doorway, she is given the promise of a son (v. 16). How deeply reminiscent this is of another woman—Sarah—standing at another doorway, hearing a prophecy concerning a child to be born to her 'in due season' (Genesis 18:10). Because of the advanced age of one or both of the partners, the reaction of both women is incredulity (Genesis 18:12; 2 Kings 4:16).

This pattern is one that is repeated in the New Testament, with the angelic prophecies to Zechariah and Mary concerning the births of John the Baptist and Jesus. These situations also carry apparently insurmountable impediments: Zechariah and Elizabeth are too old (Luke 1:18) and Mary has never had a sexual relationship (v. 34). With God, though, nothing is impossible.

Reflection

'What is impossible for mortals is possible for God' (Luke 18:27).
Is your God too small?

BARBARA MOSSE

2 KINGS 4:18–20, 32–35 (NRSV, ABRIDGED)

The Shunammite's son

When the child was older, he went out one day to his father among the reapers. He complained to his father, 'Oh, my head, my head!' The father said to his servant, 'Carry him to his mother.' He carried him and brought him to his mother; the child sat on her lap until noon, and he died... When Elisha came into the house, he saw the child lying dead on his bed. So he went in and closed the door on the two of them, and prayed to the Lord. Then he got up upon the bed and lay upon the child, putting his mouth upon his mouth, his eyes upon his eyes, and his hands upon his hands; and while he lay bent over him, the flesh of the child became warm... and the child opened his eyes.

Some years have passed since the events described in the previous reading and the promised child has now grown to boyhood. When he becomes suddenly ill and subsequently dies, the healing miracle that follows has much in common with Elijah's earlier healing of the son of the widow of Zarephath (1 Kings 17:17–24).

With the exception of the boy's father, all the action in this story is characterised by a tremendous sense of urgency. The woman wishes to be on her way to Elisha quickly (vv. 22, 24) and Elisha tells Gehazi to 'run at once to meet her' (v. 26). Gehazi is given instructions to ignore others on the road (v. 29; compare Luke 10:4). The omission of the courtesy normally extended to fellow travellers is apparently justified by the urgency of the situation.

The woman's statement that all is well (v. 26) seems to anticipate the words of Julian of Norwich, writing amid the horrors of 14th-century England. Both these women, in their different times and situations, are articulating a deep but mysterious truth, that, despite the fragility and uncertainty of life, God continues to work his purposes for good in the lives of those who love and trust him (Romans 8:28).

Reflection

'Though the fig tree does not blossom, and no fruit is on the vines...
I will exult in the God of my salvation' (Habakkuk 3:17–18).

BARBARA MOSSE

2 KINGS 4:38–41 (NRSV, ABRIDGED)

'There is death in the pot!'

When Elisha returned to Gilgal, there was a famine in the land. As the company of prophets was sitting before him, he said to his servant, 'Put the large pot on, and make some stew for the company of prophets.' One of them went out into the field to gather herbs; he found a wild vine and gathered from it a lapful of wild gourds, and came and cut them up into the pot of stew, not knowing what they were... But while they were eating the stew, they cried out, 'O man of God, there is death in the pot!' They could not eat it. He said, 'Then bring some flour.' He threw it into the pot, and said, 'Serve the people and let them eat.' And there was nothing harmful in the pot.

When Elisha returns to Gilgal, he finds the land in the grip of famine, but, by using the natural resources to hand, enough stew is made to feed him and his companions. The inadvertent addition of poisonous wild gourds to the mixture was a mistake that was, fortunately, discovered before anyone was harmed and Elisha's addition of flour detoxifies the stew (vv. 40–41). There is no indication here that the result of Elisha's actions was seen as miraculous, however; the writer simply records that the stew was now wholesome.

Whether miraculous or not, this incident offers great encouragement. How often do our own best intentions turn out to have unfortunate consequences? We may not be able to undo the damage we have inadvertently caused, but we can learn from this reading: the problem was immediately taken to Elisha, the one through whom the healing work of God flowed so strongly.

We are invited to follow this example. We are encouraged to not get caught up in a vicious and repetitive cycle of self-blame, but lay the problem quickly before our Lord, trusting in his power and will to work all things—even our mistakes—for our good and the ultimate glory of his kingdom.

Reflection

How do you respond when your actions or words inadvertently cause harm? What do you do with your feelings of guilt?

BARBARA MOSSE

2 KINGS 4:42–44 (NRSV)

Enough and to spare

A man came from Baal-shalishah, bringing food from the first fruits to the man of God; twenty loaves of barley and fresh ears of grain in his sack. Elisha said, 'Give it to the people and let them eat.' But his servant said, 'How can I set this before a hundred people?' So he repeated, 'Give it to the people and let them eat, for thus says the Lord, "They shall eat and have some left."' He set it before them, they ate, and had some left, according to the word of the Lord.

The final incident in our sequence of Elijah/Elisha stories involves a man from Baal-shalishah who brings a gift of first fruits for the man of God: 20 barley loaves and fresh ears of grain. In a clear foreshadowing of the miraculous feedings in the Gospels, Elisha orders that the food be distributed, despite the protestations of his servant that there will not be enough to feed 100 people. All are fed, however, and with food left over, 'according to the word of the Lord' (v. 44).

Through all the people and events that have been described in these four chapters, whether they are drawn in exquisite miniature detail or with broad, impressionistic brushstrokes, there is a sense of another picture inexorably coming into focus. Amid a mass of complex and often confusing historical detail, the signs pointing towards Christ and his kingdom are already present: a family is saved from ruin, the thirsty receive water, the hungry are fed and a dead child is raised to life. The message we are left with is one of great hope—that whatever the setbacks and wrong turnings caused by humanity's weakness and perversity, all will, at last, be taken up and transformed in the clear light of God's kingdom.

Reflection

'God is working his purpose out as year succeeds to year,
God is working his purpose out and the time is drawing near;
Nearer and nearer draws the time, the time that shall surely be,
When the earth shall be filled with the glory of God
as the waters cover the sea.'

Arthur Ainger, 1894

BARBARA MOSSE

Mark 9—16

In June, our daily readings took us through the first half of Mark's Gospel, up to chapter 8. Now, as we return to Mark, we shall follow Jesus to the end of this Gospel, to crucifixion, burial and an empty tomb. At the point where we start to read, the mood of Mark's story has just changed. Jesus has spoken of his coming death and warned his friends that the way ahead will be demanding and difficult: 'If any want to become my followers, let them deny themselves and take up their cross' (8:34). This will not be a comfortable journey.

In chapters 9 and 10, we watch Jesus and his disciples making their way from Galilee to Jerusalem. Often we pause, to watch Jesus in conversation or hear him teach. With friends and strangers, he speaks about the values of God's kingdom, about how people treat one another and about the way of discipleship. These are words for us, too. As readers we are drawn into the story, confronted with its challenges and invited to draw its teaching into our lives.

When Jesus reaches Jerusalem, the mood changes. The crowds are glad, but the city's leaders find him a disturbing and awkward presence. Chapters 11 and 12 are full of tense and prickly conversation, sharp questions and cryptic replies. Big issues are in focus—death, money, God's law and, especially, Jesus' authority.

At Mark 13, Helen Julian takes over the commentary. That chapter is like a periscope in the story: Jesus looks upwards and ahead and speaks of promise and judgment. Then we return to the gathering gloom, as chapters 14 and 15 tell the story of his passion. Events move swiftly and dreadfully on—from arrest and trial to scourging and crucifixion—until, one dark afternoon, the temple curtain splits and Jesus breathes out his life: 'Truly this man was God's Son' (15:39). It is a strange sort of good news, for Jesus is known most clearly not by what he says but by what he suffers and not through his doing but through his dying. The wood of death becomes a tree of life. The place of darkness is a source of light for the world.

John Proctor

MARK 9:2–5, 7 (NRSV)

More than a martyr

Six days later, Jesus took with him Peter and James and John, and led them up a high mountain apart, by themselves. And he was transfigured before them, and his clothes became dazzling white, such as no one on earth could bleach them. And there appeared to them Elijah with Moses, who were talking with Jesus. Then Peter said to Jesus, 'Rabbi, it is good for us to be here: let us make three dwellings, one for you, one for Moses, and one for Elijah.'... Then a cloud overshadowed them, and from the cloud there came a voice, 'This is my Son, the Beloved; listen to him!'

Just before this, Jesus has spoken of suffering ahead (8:31). Now his transfiguration sets the hardship in perspective. The world may despise Jesus as an executed criminal, puzzle over the tragedy of his dying or honour him as a holy martyr, but he is much more than this. He is in contact with the life of heaven and the glory of God. He is the hub and heart of God's work across the years. Saints and seers from Israel's past witness to his greatness. As the voice sounds from above, we recognise Jesus as God's beloved Son.

Peter wanted to freeze the moment. Constructing shelters would help to preserve the occasion, like a family photo album, but this was not to be. The disciples had something more important to learn and do: 'Listen to him!' said the voice of God. Jesus would lead them down the mountain and they must trust and follow. Even when he took his friends into difficult places, he would be about God's purpose and within God's love.

This evening will bring the closing ceremony of the Olympic Games. Fireworks will light up the sky, famous faces will parade around the track and the display will be beamed across the world. By contrast, the transfiguration was a very private lightshow. It was more to do with faith than fame.

Prayer

Lord Jesus Christ, please give us a fuller sense of your glory, so that we may follow your way with commitment and courage.

JOHN PROCTOR

Monday 13 August

Mark 9:38–41 (NRSV)

The Spirit blows

> John said to [Jesus], 'Teacher, we saw someone casting out demons in your name, and we tried to stop him, because he was not following us.' But Jesus said, 'Do not stop him; for no one who does a deed of power in my name will be able soon afterwards to speak evil of me. Whoever is not against us is for us. For truly I tell you, whoever gives you a cup of water to drink because you bear the name of Christ will by no means lose the reward.'

The twelve disciples were a tight little group. They got to know each other well as they travelled, but Jesus made a much wider impact, too. Many people heard and welcomed his teaching and the after-effects of his preaching tours would have been lively and varied. It appears that the strange exorcist in this story had gained some sort of healing ministry from his contact with Jesus. He was not, so far as we can tell, claiming credit himself. It was all done in Jesus' name.

The disciples were suspicious. This man did not belong to their group. They came back to Jesus with questions and concerns. Was it all right for someone outside their immediate circle to use 'your name' (v. 38)? But Jesus was positive. If people used his name to bring hope and healing in the world, he would not object. He would welcome friends and allies wherever he found them.

The fresh air of the Spirit still blows freely and sometimes in unexpected places. God does do new things and will not always work through the traditional patterns of Church life. Yet Christians are sometimes anxious and suspicious, as the disciples were. The untidy and unfamiliar alarm us. We like to be sure that all is proper and ordered. With this in mind, perhaps the key word from our reading is 'name' (vv. 38, 39, 41)—the name of Jesus. Good deeds done for his sake always deserve our support.

Prayer

Lord Jesus Christ, help me to see what you are doing in this world and encourage the people who are doing it with you.

John Proctor

MARK 10:13–16 (NRSV)

Infant school

> People were bringing little children to [Jesus] in order that he might touch them; and the disciples spoke sternly to them. But when Jesus saw this, he was indignant and said to them, 'Let the little children come to me; do not stop them; for it is to such as these that the kingdom of God belongs. Truly I tell you, whoever does not receive the kingdom of God as a little child will never enter it.' And he took them up in his arms, laid his hands on them, and blessed them.

Oh dear! Jesus' followers get it wrong again—keeping Jesus to themselves, protecting him from the public, blocking the path and missing the way of the kingdom. In Mark's Gospel, the road of Christian service is strewn with mistakes and misunderstandings. The disciples have to learn from the tangles they get into and the times they go astray. I find this encouraging; it gives the rest of us hope. Jesus will not give up on us, even when we are not holy, kind or wise. Sometimes we learn best by stumbling and tumbling.

Jesus often dealt with the world in unexpected ways. He called not the righteous but sinners (2:17). He spent time with the crowd rather than his own family (3:35). He rejoiced in a widow's mite more than in richer and grander gifts (12:44). He said that little children can pilot the rest of us into God's kingdom (10:14–15). Humility and dependence come more easily to them. They do not have the baggage of pride and self-importance that adults often pick up. They know they have to trust; they realise they need a love greater than themselves.

Of course, children have much to learn, but they also have important things to teach. They remind us not just of how we were but also how we could be in our walk with God. Happy is the church, or the home, where children and adults can help each other to follow the Christian way.

Prayer

Pray for children you know—for their safety and joy amid the challenges and opportunities of their young years.

JOHN PROCTOR

MARK 10:28–31 (NRSV)

Prosperity gospel?

> Peter began to say to [Jesus], 'Look, we have left everything and followed you.' Jesus said, 'Truly I tell you, there is no one who has left house or brothers or sisters or mother or father or children or fields, for my sake and the sake of the good news, who will not receive a hundredfold now in this age—houses, brothers and sisters, mothers and children, and fields, with persecutions—and in the age to come eternal life. But many who are first will be last, and the last will be first.'

This is the tail end of a conversation about property. It started when a rich man came to Jesus (v. 17). When the man went away, Jesus started to talk of how wealth can get between people and God (v. 23). Eventually, Peter interrupted, 'But Jesus, we haven't got any wealth. We've left it all, to follow you.'

Peter was right. Some of the disciples had walked away from a steady job. Others had set aside, for a while at least, family duties or business commitments. Jesus himself had left a settled pattern of life. Where would it all lead? So, Jesus speaks here about his vision for community, the big family of faith he is starting to shape. He warns of persecutions and promises his friends that their road will have a destination. God's best and richest blessings are ahead.

'Leaving everything' was Jesus' call to a few people. Even then, this was not for everyone and it isn't for everyone today. Yet, in some lands, Christian faith does involve major sacrifices. Coming to Christ can set a person at odds with family or make it harder to find a job or even endanger personal safety.

Christians in these places are our brothers and sisters. They need our prayers and sometimes they ask the Church in the West for more than prayer alone—for material help, support for their human rights or, occasionally, refugee status in a safer land.

Reflection

Where do you hear of Christians facing persecution today?
What might we do to help and encourage some of these people?

JOHN PROCTOR

MARK 10:42–45 (NRSV)

Servant kingdom

> Jesus called them and said to them, 'You know that among the Gentiles those whom they recognise as their rulers lord it over them, and their great ones are tyrants over them. But it is not so among you; but whoever wishes to become great among you must be your servant, and whoever wishes to be first among you must be slave of all. For the Son of Man came not to be served but to serve, and to give his life a ransom for many.'

Throughout the Gospels, two themes are woven together. One is the identity and nature of Jesus: who he is and what he has come to do. The second is the kind of life to which he calls his followers and the sort of community he intends them to become. Both themes are present in today's reading. As usual, they are connected. The way we live reflects the Lord we trust; Christians put the life of Christ into practice.

Jesus' community is a servant people. We are not meant to deal in pride or power, nor strive for status. Where there is work to do, a need to meet or help to give, there the friends of Christ are called to show the love of Christ. Just as he 'emptied himself, taking the form of a slave' (Philippians 2:7), his people, too, will be generous, humble and helpful. The Church is called to be a community with its sleeves rolled up, ready for service, even when that service is menial or messy. Jesus gave himself, in life and death, for the sake of others. He asks us to follow his way.

This strikes me as a liberating word. Serving one another is something that we can all do. It is a mark of the Church and it is a mark that all the members can help to make. Practical service can bind a congregation together, strongly and joyfully, and help us understand more of the love of Jesus.

Reflection

Lord Jesus, what can I do, to help my church serve more truly and gladly in your name?

JOHN PROCTOR

MARK 10:46–47, 51–52 (NRSV)

A shout in the street

> [Jesus and his followers] came to Jericho. As he and his disciples and a large crowd were leaving Jericho, Bartimaeus son of Timaeus, a blind beggar, was sitting by the roadside. When he heard that it was Jesus of Nazareth, he began to shout out and say, 'Jesus, Son of David, have mercy on me!'... Then Jesus said to him, 'What do you want me to do for you?' The blind man said to him, 'My teacher, let me see again.' Jesus said to him, 'Go; your faith has made you well.' Immediately he regained his sight and followed him on the way.

Jericho was the last staging post for pilgrims. After one more day's walking, Jesus would see Jerusalem, but Bartimaeus could not see at all. He had to *listen* for passing travellers—their movement, their tread, conversation—and live from their gifts. The commotion of the crowd walking with Jesus would have quickly caught his attention. Bartimaeus had heard of this man and wanted to meet him.

'Son of David' (v. 47) is a royal title. It casts Jesus as the Lord's anointed, as Israel's promised Messiah. It speaks of God's kingdom coming. We sometimes hear this title in the Gospels when Jesus is healing, for, like David, Jesus was a shepherd king. He cared for people, as shepherds have to care for their flocks. Like a shepherd, he looked out for the wounded, the wandering and the weak. He wanted to set them right and help them find new wholeness.

Bartimaeus certainly discovered a fuller way of life. Quite what he was thinking when he said 'Son of David' we may never know, but he knew enough to shout loudly and ask for sight. Then, once he could see, he followed. He had seen enough to seek, trusted enough to follow and believed enough to go with Jesus on the road. Blind Bartimaeus? I think not. This man saw some important things very clearly indeed.

Prayer

In some parts of the world, diseases of the eye are easy to catch and hard to cure. Pray for good medical care to reach these places and the people who most need it.

JOHN PROCTOR

MARK 11:1–2, 7–10 (NRSV, ABRIDGED)

King's highway

When [Jesus and his followers] were approaching Jerusalem, at Bethphage and Bethany, near the Mount of Olives, he sent two of his disciples and said to them, 'Go into the village ahead of you and... you will find tied there a colt...' Then they brought the colt to Jesus and threw their cloaks on it; and he sat on it. Many people spread their cloaks on the road, and others spread leafy branches that they had cut in the fields. Then those who went ahead and those who followed were shouting, 'Hosanna! Blessed is the one who comes in the name of the Lord! Blessed is the coming kingdom of our ancestor David!'

The Mount of Olives is quite a steep ridge, overlooking Jerusalem. Going east, the ground falls quickly away towards Jericho and the Jordan valley. To the west, the pilgrim road leads downhill towards Jerusalem and the temple. Jesus had come up from Jericho. Now he would ride down the Mount into Jerusalem, on a young donkey.

Jesus had contacts in Bethany; I suspect he borrowed the animal he mentions here from friends. The point of this incident is not where the donkey came from, however, but where it took Jesus—the impact he had and the image he created by entering the city this way.

It is a gentle scene. On such a small beast, Jesus was among the crowds, not high above them. There is no great impression of power or force. This was not a military parade, but it was enough to cause excitement. A line in the Old Testament (Zechariah 9:9) speaks of a king coming on a donkey's colt. I wonder if Jesus deliberately fulfilled the prophecy to make a point to the people.

If this was his intention, the crowd surely got the message as they shouted psalms of freedom and praise. 'Hosanna' means 'save us', but Jesus was taking his time. He rode into the city, looked around the temple, then went off to Bethany to rest (Mark 11:11). He had big concerns on his mind. He was acting with authority, but without haste.

Prayer

Pray for anyone you know who has big decisions to make or strong pressures to face.

JOHN PROCTOR

MARK 11:15–17 (NRSV)

Turning tables

Then [Jesus and his followers] came to Jerusalem. And he entered the temple and began to drive out those who were selling and those who were buying in the temple, and he overturned the tables of the money-changers and the seats of those who sold doves; and he would not allow anyone to carry anything through the temple. He was teaching and saying, 'Is it not written, "My house shall be called a house of prayer for all the nations"? But you have made it a den of robbers.'

We are not used to Jesus being angry. The church talks more about his gentler moods, but the incident in the temple is, by any reckoning, an angry scene. Jesus does not like what he finds and makes quite a little explosion amid the traders and their tables. It was not a full-scale riot. If it had been, Roman troops would have intervened. Even so, as Jesus banged furniture about and scattered coins across the floor, he would have caused quite a commotion.

What bothered him? It may have been a matter of money getting in the way of prayer. Some Jewish writings of this period tell of inflated prices for sacrificial animals and of large revenues that found their way to Jerusalem's richest families. If Jesus encountered this, it would surely have angered him to think of poor pilgrims being ripped off. The text he quoted about 'prayer for all nations' (v. 17) might be a complaint about traders occupying the one area of the temple where Gentiles could pray.

It seems that Jesus had all this in mind after his tour of the temple the previous day. When he upset the furniture, he was launching a protest. He wanted worship to be more accessible and open, to the poor, the humble and the stranger.

What about our worship? How easy is it for people to find their way into our churches and feel at home there? What would Jesus think of the welcome we give to poor people, foreigners and strangers? That, it seems, was his concern in Jerusalem.

Prayer

Lord Jesus, our church is your church.
Help us to please you in what we do there.

JOHN PROCTOR

MARK 12:14–17 (NRSV, ABRIDGED)

Tax dodge?

[Some Pharisees and Herodians] came and said to [Jesus], 'Teacher, we know that you are sincere, and show deference to no one... Is it lawful to pay taxes to the emperor, or not...?' But knowing their hypocrisy, he said to them, 'Why are you putting me to the test? Bring me a denarius and let me see it.'... Then he said to them, 'Whose head is this, and whose title?' They answered, 'The emperor's.' Jesus said to them, 'Give to the emperor the things that are the emperor's, and to God the things that are God's.'

Several scenes in this phase of the Gospel start with people questioning Jesus. Taxes raised an obvious problem. Nobody likes paying them anyway, but it is worse when a foreign government is involved. Even more disturbing in this encounter, the coins represented the emperor as a god and Israel had a law against graven images (Exodus 20:4). What would Jesus say? Would he declare himself a rebel (if he answered 'No') or a faithless collaborator (if he said 'Yes')? Either way his opponents could make trouble for him.

Jesus' answer seems evasive, but perhaps his point was that there will never be an easy answer. People of faith have often lived under difficult regimes and there really is no simple rule about how God relates to government. Christians will always have to think about loyalty and conscience, as times change and new issues arise. What is the State entitled to claim and where might my responsibility to Christ cut across the law of the land? Over the centuries, some highly respected Christians have defied civil power in the name of God. I am writing this in the USA, just a few miles from Martin Luther King's grave.

'Whose head is this?' said Jesus (v. 16). 'Whose image?' would be a more accurate translation. Image matters a lot, for you and I are made in God's image (Genesis 1:27), so we ought to put God first. This first and greatest commitment will shape all the loyalties and loves of our living.

Prayer

Pray for the people who manage public finance in your local community, that they will be wise, careful and honest.

JOHN PROCTOR

Mark 12:41–44 (NRSV)

Cheerful giver

[Jesus] sat down opposite the treasury, and watched the crowd putting money into the treasury. Many rich people put in large sums. A poor widow came and put in two small copper coins, which are worth a penny. Then he called his disciples and said to them, 'Truly I tell you, this poor widow has put in more than all those who are contributing to the treasury. For all of them have contributed out of their abundance; but she out of her poverty has put in everything she had, all she had to live on.'

The translation 'worth a penny' is near the mark. The widow's gift represents a tiny fraction of a normal day's wage, yet, for some people, even this small sum would make a difference to a day's living. If giving is measured by what a person has left over, then she had given generously indeed, for her giving had cut into her daily survival, into the iron rations that kept her alive.

There were several trumpet-shaped offering boxes in the temple in Jerusalem. It is probable that large gifts would have made a resonant rattle as they tumbled their way down. The widow's coins would have fallen more gently, yet, for Jesus, her gift spoke loudly, declaring that here was a heart and life devoted to God. He valued what she had offered above the larger gifts of wealthier people.

In different ways, our last three readings have all been to do with the subject of money. The Bible warns against the 'love of money' (1 Timothy 6:10), but even without loving it, we must live with it and use it as well as possible. Giving is part of that stewardship. To give is a privilege (Acts 20:35) and God loves it when we give gladly (2 Corinthians 9:7). People who are generous out of limited resources are a shining example to the rest of us. We should thank God for them. Jesus surely did.

Prayer

Remember people who have been generous to you in the course of the years. Thank God for them, and for the difference they have made to your life.

John Proctor

MARK 13:5–8 (NRSV)

Stay calm and carry on

Then Jesus began to say to [his followers], 'Beware that no one leads you astray. Many will come in my name and say "I am he!" and they will lead many astray. When you hear of wars and rumours of wars, do not be alarmed; this must take place, but the end is still to come. For nation will rise against nation, and kingdom against kingdom; there will be earthquakes in various places; there will be famines. This is but the beginning of the birth pangs.'

This is a pivotal point in Mark's Gospel. Until now, Jesus has been journeying towards Jerusalem. In the previous chapter, he finally arrived and, at the beginning of chapter 13, he shocked his disciples by speaking of the destruction of the temple. Mark uses that brief story to introduce a chapter of teaching on the end of the world. Commentators vary in how they understand this chapter. Some see it as apocalyptic—about the end of the world as a whole—while others see it as being addressed to the Church under persecution.

Whichever the case, these verses give us the big picture of global events and, sadly, they are still very familiar. As I write, I could put names to the wars and earthquakes and famines, and see the news pictures. It is a little harder to bring to mind those saying that they are Jesus, though it still happens, too. In Mark's time, there were those claiming to be the Messiah (thus denying that Jesus had been) and those claiming to be Jesus himself, returned from heaven to usher in the end.

It was natural that Christians under persecution would wait eagerly for their vindication, but Jesus is shown commending patience. These events are part of God's plan (the word 'must' (v. 7) points to God's purposes being worked out), but they are only the beginning of labour, not the birth itself.

The second letter to the Thessalonians, especially chapter 2, is a good companion to this passage, addressed as it is to those convinced the end had already arrived. Jesus asks us to trust God and not to be alarmed.

Prayer

Lord, give me patience as I wait for your purposes to be worked out.

HELEN JULIAN CSF

MARK 13:32–37 (NRSV)

Staying awake

[Jesus said] 'But about that day or hour no one knows, neither the angels in heaven, nor the Son, but only the Father. Beware, keep alert; for you do not know when the time will come. It is like a man going on a journey, when he leaves home and puts his slaves in charge, each with his work, and commands the doorkeeper to be on the watch. Therefore, keep awake—for you do not know when the master of the house will come, in the evening, or at midnight, or at cockcrow, or at dawn, or else he may find you asleep when he comes suddenly. And what I say to you I say to all: keep awake.'

It feels strange to hear these words in August. Verses 35–37 are the set reading for Night Prayer in my community in Advent, as we move towards Christmas, anticipating the joyful birth of Jesus. Here, the context is rather darker. As we saw yesterday, Mark, in chapter 13, collects Jesus' teaching about the end, about persecution and suffering, disasters natural and man-made.

The end of these things is not dark, however; it is the coming again of Christ, the second coming in power and triumph of the child who came in weakness to Bethlehem. He comes to 'gather his elect' (v. 27).

Naturally, we want to know when this great event will happen—we want to be ready—but Jesus' teaching is more challenging: no one knows except the Father and, therefore, being ready must be our default position. We must live each day as if it were the last one, while knowing that it may not be, living in the 'now' and the 'not yet' of the kingdom.

Jesus' acknowledgment that not even he knows the time of the end has caused theologians much difficulty over the centuries—if he and the Father are one, how can he not know? This may be an indication of an authentic saying: why would the church invent something so difficult? His teaching is clear, though: keep alert, stay awake. It is a message for all people in all times.

Reflection

How do you juggle living now while also looking towards the end?

HELEN JULIAN CSF

MARK 14:3–8 (NRSV, ABRIDGED)

Extravagant love

While [Jesus] was at Bethany… a woman came with an alabaster jar of very costly ointment of nard, and she broke open the jar and poured the ointment on his head. But some were there who said to one another in anger, 'Why was the ointment wasted in this way? For this ointment could have been sold for more than three hundred denarii, and the money given to the poor.' And they scolded her. But Jesus said, 'Let her alone; why do you trouble her? She has performed a good service for me. For you always have the poor with you, and you can show kindness to them whenever you wish; but you will not always have me. She has done what she could; she has anointed my body beforehand for its burial.'

Mark often makes 'sandwiches' of his stories and this is the 'filling'—tomorrow we will look at the 'bread'.

The story of a woman anointing Jesus is found in all four Gospels, though in different contexts, which affect its meaning. In Matthew and Mark, the woman anoints Jesus' head, while Luke and John have her anointing his feet. The word Messiah means 'anointed one' and anointing the head with oil is associated with kingship (2 Kings 9:6). So, Mark depicts the woman as recognising Jesus' true identity. A detail found only in Mark is that she 'broke open the jar', which implies that she used all its contents, holding nothing back. This was not a carefully measured ritual, but an extravagant gesture.

Although some of those who saw it were critical, Jesus defends the woman. It could sound as though he is saying poverty is never going to be solved, but that is putting a sociological interpretation on a saying which is actually Christological. The darker side of the story follows. As opposition to Jesus grows, he is in increasing danger of his life. The woman has anointed him as Messiah, but also as one who is soon to die. This anonymous woman, in her extravagant love, has a deeper insight than the religious experts around her.

Prayer

Jesus, help me to recognise you and set me free
to pour out all my love for you.

HELEN JULIAN CSF

MARK 14:1–2, 10–11 (NRSV)

Fear, greed and betrayal

It was two days before the Passover and the festival of Unleavened Bread. The chief priests and the scribes were looking for a way to arrest Jesus by stealth and kill him; for they said, 'Not during the festival, or there may be a riot among the people.' ... Then Judas Iscariot, who was one of the twelve, went to the chief priests in order to betray him to them. When they heard it, they were greatly pleased, and promised to give him money. So he began to look for an opportunity to betray him.

These verses come before and after the story of the anointing at Bethany—the 'bread' of this particular 'sandwich'. As is often the case with this construction in Mark's Gospel, the stories shed light on one another. One commentator describes them as a canvas with three sections, with the darker pictures on the left and right changing the meaning of the bright central image.

Jerusalem would have been packed with pilgrims. Passover, celebrating liberation from slavery in Egypt, was combined with the spring agricultural festival of Unleavened Bread and drew huge crowds. The religious authorities are canny enough to see the dangers—Jesus has a following and arresting him too openly could spark a riot. This, in turn, would cause problems with the Roman authorities. So, Judas' offer is very welcome. If he can tell them where to find Jesus, in some quiet place and time, they can both deal with this troublemaker *and* keep the peace.

It is hard to be sure about Judas' motives. Mark mentions money, but this is only offered to him after he has already come to the priests. Other evangelists say his motive was greed (Matthew 26:15), Satan (Luke 22:3) and Satan plus a habit of stealing (John 13:2; 12:6). Perhaps the uncertainty shows just how difficult it is to know why people do what is wrong. The word 'betray' (Mark 14:11), which can also be translated as 'hand over' or 'deliver up', has theological overtones for Mark. Judas' treachery, mysteriously, is not outside God's plan and purpose. God can use both the woman's devotion and Judas' betrayal.

Reflection

Can you remember a time when something that seemed to be a disaster looked different in retrospect?

HELEN JULIAN CSF

MARK 14:22–26 (NRSV)

Breaking bread, sharing wine

While they were eating, [Jesus] took a loaf of bread, and after blessing it he broke it, gave it to them, and said, 'Take; this is my body.' Then he took a cup, and after giving thanks he gave it to them, and all of them drank from it. He said to them, 'This is my blood of the covenant, which is poured out for many. Truly I tell you, I will never again drink of the fruit of the vine until that day when I drink it new in the kingdom of God.' When they had sung the hymn, they went out to the Mount of Olives.

On this Sunday, as on every Sunday, millions of Christians around the world will be taking bread and wine, blessing them and sharing them together. It is one of the things that make it very hard to read this passage and the equivalents in the other Gospels without superimposing on them how the churches have interpreted and used them, and remembering all the controversies over the centuries about this key Christian religious act.

Mark's account of the last supper is very brief and starkly simple. It looks back to the other meals that Jesus had shared during his ministry, often with those disapproved of by the respectable (2:16). It also looks forward to the longed-for kingdom of God.

The 'blood of the covenant' also looks back to the Old Testament covenant, sealed with blood (Exodus 24:8). This new covenant, however, is now made with all people, not just the chosen people of the old covenant—the word translated 'many' has the sense of 'all' not just one or a few.

It is a powerful picture of Jesus' self-giving love, as he offers to those whom he loves and who love him his very life, his body and blood, symbolised by bread and wine. Even at this moment of great tension, as he looks towards his death, he prays a prayer of blessing and then offers his disciples hope that death will not be the end, even as they make their way to Gethsemane.

Reflection

What does the Eucharist mean for you?

HELEN JULIAN CSF

MARK 14:53, 60–62 (NRSV)

Who are you?

They took Jesus to the high priest; and all the chief priests, the elders, and the scribes were assembled… Then the high priest stood up before them and asked Jesus, 'Have you no answer? What is it that they testify against you?' But he was silent and did not answer. Again the high priest asked him, 'Are you the Messiah, the Son of the Blessed One?' Jesus said, 'I am; and "you will see the Son of Man seated at the right hand of the Power", and "coming with the clouds of heaven".'

We fast-forward through the agony in the garden of Gethsemane, the betrayal of Jesus by Judas and the fear of the disciples as they desert him. After the gentle equality and sharing of the last supper and the poignancy of Jesus' prayer in the garden, we have moved into a different world—a world of power, falsehood and interrogation.

The religious authorities—as is sadly often the case—are afraid of the new teaching; their first instinct is to try to stop it. The testimonies to which they demand an answer are false and disagree with one another (vv. 56–59), so there is no need for Jesus to answer them, but his silence also fulfils Old Testament texts (Isaiah 53:7; Psalm 38:13–15)—passages that were applied to the expected Messiah.

Hence, the high priest's question is not unexpected—it combines titles for Jesus already used in Mark's Gospel ('Messiah' in 8:29; 'Son' in 1:11 and 9:7) and paves the way for his simple but earth-shattering statement 'I am'—which is not only an acceptance of these titles but also a reference to the phrase used by God in the Old Testament to identify himself (most famously in Exodus 3:14, but also in Deuteronomy 32:39 and Isaiah 41:4 and 43:10).

Jesus goes on to quote two further Old Testament texts that he has already used—Psalm 110:1 (Mark 12:36) and Daniel 7:13 (Mark 13:26). They speak of the Messiah and now he takes them to himself. No wonder he is a threat to the religious authorities; he takes their own words and gives them a new meaning.

Prayer

Jesus, open my eyes to see you as Messiah and Beloved Son.

HELEN JULIAN CSF

MARK 15:9–15 (NRSV)

Power misused

Then [Pilate] answered [the crowd], 'Do you want me to release for you the King of the Jews?' For he realised that it was out of jealousy that the chief priests had handed him over. But the chief priests stirred up the crowd to have him release Barabbas for them instead. Pilate spoke to them again, 'Then what do you wish me to do with the man you call the King of the Jews?' They shouted back, 'Crucify him!' Pilate asked them, 'Why, what evil has he done?' But they shouted all the more, 'Crucify him!' So Pilate, wishing to satisfy the crowd, released Barabbas for them; and after flogging Jesus, he handed him over to be crucified.

The religious authorities have found Jesus guilty of a religious charge, but they do not have the power to put him to death, so they need to enlist the help of Pilate, representative of the hated Roman colonial power. Mark gives no account of a second 'trial' by Pilate, although the charge has now become a political one—Jesus is no longer the Messiah, but the King of the Jews and, hence, potentially a threat to the State.

In John's Gospel, Pilate asks, 'What is truth?' (John 18:38), but truth does not seem very important in this murky story of competing power blocs, united only by their common fear of one who seems to undermine both religious and secular power. It does not really matter whether the charge is valid or not, only that the present religious system can continue undisturbed and Jerusalem remains peaceful and firmly under Pilate's rule.

Pilate is shown as weak. Perhaps a little unconvinced by the chief priests' case, he gives the final say to the crowd—'Jesus or Barabbas? Who shall die and who shall live?' The crowd, as often happens, is easily swayed and so the murderer is released and the Lord of life goes to his death.

Power is still misused today, with popular opinion counting for more than truth or justice. It is a very modern story and one still happening wherever power is not rooted in compassion and love.

Prayer

Give me courage to do the right thing in the face of competing pressures.

HELEN JULIAN CSF

MARK 15:25, 33–34, 37–39 (NRSV)

A life-changing death

It was nine o'clock in the morning when they crucified him... When it was noon, darkness came over the whole land until three in the afternoon. At three o'clock Jesus cried out with a loud voice, 'Eloi, Eloi, lema sabachthani?' which means, 'My God, my God, why have you forsaken me?'... Then Jesus gave a loud cry and breathed his last. And the curtain of the temple was torn in two, from top to bottom. Now when the centurion, who stood facing him, saw that in this way he breathed his last, he said, 'Truly this man was God's Son!'

Jesus has shared human life to the full—birth, work, friendship, suffering, betrayal. Now he shares in death, too. It is, at one and the same time, very ordinary and extraordinary. This death is, as all deaths are, rooted in time and space. It is a real human individual who hangs on the cross, suffers and dies. The only words that Mark records are those of abandonment—Jesus shares even in this. They are the words that begin Psalm 22, which ends with an expression of trust in God. Such trust does not rule out Jesus having a real sense of having been forsaken by his Father.

It is also an extraordinary death and one that has extraordinary consequences. There is darkness at a time when there is no reason for it (the suggestion that it was an eclipse does not hold water, as that cannot happen when the moon is full, which would have been the case at Passover). Jesus dies far more quickly than would have been expected and, strangest of all, at the moment of his death, the curtain in the temple that divided the holy place from the holy of holies (Exodus 26:33) is torn in two. The old covenant is over because it has been fulfilled and a new way to God is opened up.

The centurion's confession is perhaps the first fruits of this new way—a Gentile believes purely because of how he sees Jesus die. There is no miracle, no power, no teaching, just a human death that changes all death for ever.

Reflection

As you gaze on Jesus on the cross, who do you see?

HELEN JULIAN CSF

MARK 15:42–43, 46–47 (NRSV, ABRIDGED)

Dead and buried

When evening had come, and since it was the day of Preparation... Joseph of Arimathea, a respected member of the council, who was also himself waiting expectantly for the kingdom of God, went boldly to Pilate and asked for the body of Jesus. Then Joseph bought a linen cloth, and taking down the body, wrapped it in the linen cloth, and laid it in a tomb that had been hewn out of the rock. He then rolled a stone against the door of the tomb. Mary Magdalene and Mary the mother of Joses saw where the body was laid.

'Dead and buried' we say of something—a plan, idea, relationship or part of our life—that is definitely over. Not just dead, but also buried.

Burying the dead was a duty under Jewish Law, a duty that conflicted with the Roman custom of leaving the bodies of criminals unburied. Joseph of Arimathea is treating Jesus as if he were a close member of his own family in taking responsibility for his burial.

Joseph is an intriguing figure. This is the only story in which he appears and Mark does not say that he was a follower of Jesus. Perhaps it was only because he was not identified with Jesus that he could take the risk of asking for the body. Maybe it was because he was, in fact, a *secret* follower that he was willing to take that risk. Matthew says he was (27:57); Luke (23:50–51) says that although he was a member of the religious council that condemned Jesus, he had not consented to it. Perhaps this concern for his good name shows that, whatever his position at the time of the crucifixion, he later became a member of the Christian community, finding in this 'criminal' what he had been waiting for.

Whatever the reality, Jesus is buried. His own disciples have forsaken him, but someone steps forward to do this last service. In the shadows of the story are the women who stayed at the cross and still cannot abandon him, even when all hope seems to be dead and buried.

Prayer

Lord of life, when my hopes seem dead and buried,
let me keep faith like the women.

HELEN JULIAN CSF

MARK 16:2, 5–8 (NRSV, ABRIDGED)

Ending and beginning

Very early on the first day of the week, when the sun had risen, [the women] went to the tomb... As they entered the tomb, they saw a young man, dressed in a white robe, sitting on the right side; and they were alarmed. But he said to them, 'Do not be alarmed; you are looking for Jesus of Nazareth, who was crucified. He has been raised; he is not here... But go, tell his disciples and Peter that he is going ahead of you to Galilee; there you will see him, just as he told you.' So they went out and fled from the tomb, for terror and amazement had seized them; and they said nothing to anyone, for they were afraid.

It is an extraordinary way to end a book and commentators disagree entirely with each other about whether this is the original end to Mark's Gospel or not. Some believe that, because the resurrection stories would have been well known in the community for which Mark wrote, there was no need to record them. Perhaps Mark wrote a longer ending that has been lost. Whatever the truth, it reminds us that the Gospel writers not only record but also shape their material according to the story they seek to tell.

There seems now no way of knowing Mark's intentions, so we must wrestle with the story as we have it. The white robe marks out the young man as a heavenly being—a messenger from God—and it is God and God's power that are emphasised. 'He has been raised' prompts the question, 'By whom?' The resurrection is God's act of power.

Jesus is always on the move, going ahead—he has gone ahead through death and now goes ahead into a new and unimaginable life, which begins in the familiarity of Galilee. In this he fulfils his own prophecy in 14:28.

The women's fear is understandable. New life is often terrifying and it can be easier to stay mourning than 'go', but this is the promise of the resurrection—how will we respond?

Reflection

Is there a place in your life where you choose to stay mourning rather than to 'go' into new life?

HELEN JULIAN CSF

The BRF

Magazine

Order Forms

The Managing Editor writes...

From this issue onward, I shall be introducing the BRF Magazine in my role as Managing Editor. I oversee all four series of BRF's Bible reading notes—*New Daylight*, *Guidelines*, *Day by Day with God* and *The Upper Room*—working with the various Commissioning Editors to help our readers to nurture a love of scripture and a daily engagement with its message.

As Richard Fisher explained in the previous issue, 2012 sees the 90th anniversary of BRF's ministry as a provider of Bible reading resources. With the Diamond Jubilee of Queen Elizabeth II also being celebrated in June, and all the excitement surrounding the Olympic Games, there is much to enjoy this year.

We can be thankful to God that our work continues to expand, deepening the faith of adults and children in local settings—within the family at home, and in schools and churches—and much further afield, as our printed and digital resources, not to mention Messy Church, reach people on an international scale.

With all this growth and new opportunities for ministry close to home and far away, it's important to remember that the powerhouse for everything we do is 'Christ in [us], the hope of glory' (Colossians 1:27). As the cheers die away in the Olympic arenas, as many of us troop back to work after our extended Jubilee Bank Holiday, and as BRF looks forward to its next decade, we continue to 'struggle with all the energy that he powerfully inspires' within us (v. 29).

In this issue of the BRF Magazine, Mark Chester and Lucy Moore encourage us to think about the ways in which sport and competition can bring people together to flourish as united communities, while an extract from Michael Mitton's book *Dreaming of Home* takes a more contemplative route, looking at 'how we can adventure into our own souls'. Wherever you are on your spiritual journey, we hope that BRF can help you reach your goal.

Lisa Cherrett
Managing Editor, Bible reading notes

Winner takes all?

Mark Chester

It's been a long wait, but at last the Olympic Games are upon us. There are now so many sports on the Olympic programme that most people will find something to interest them. Although I could happily watch any of the events, for me, the Games are primarily about athletics, and the contests I will not miss are the men's and women's 100m sprint finals—in my opinion the purest sporting competitions there are.

I mean 'purest' in the sense that the 100m sprint is easy to understand and uncontaminated by excessive rules. You start at one point, run as fast as you can and finish at another. I love the simplicity of it, and I think that my affection for it is partly because it mirrors the first sporting event that I ever competed in—namely, the race to the next lamp post!

In my life, the challenge 'I'll race you to the next lamp post' was most commonly issued by or to my father, brother and friends, and the motive behind the suggestion was never just a desire to win. It was more about doing something that was fun, something that would make us laugh and would satisfy us, regardless of who came first. It was for the joy of taking part. Clearly, the motive of the participants in an Olympic 100m sprint final is slightly different: they each want to win a gold medal and be crowned the fastest man or woman on the planet.

> *... to win a gold medal and be crowned the fastest man or woman on the planet*

Is this motivation inevitable? Perhaps. But was it intended? Perhaps not. The founder of the modern Olympic Movement, Pierre de Coubertin, expressed his philosophy for the Games in what is now the Olympic Creed:

The most important thing in the Olympic Games is not to win but to take part, just as the most important thing in life is not the triumph but the struggle. The essential thing is not to have conquered but to have fought well.

Coubertin used the Games to develop three universal values reflecting this creed, which could be applied not just to sport but to society as a whole—principles that, I believe, apply equally in our lives as Christians.

Respect

The principle of fair play is crucial to the success of the Olympic Games because without it the competition is meaningless. Likewise, our achievements in life are meaningless unless we maintain our integrity. How do we do that? The following words of Jesus below make it clear. In my opinion, no one has ever summed up the meaning of fair play as effectively as Jesus did when he spoke these words:

… nobody is excluded from the privilege of receiving the grace of God

'So in everything, do to others what you would have them do to you, for this sums up the Law and the Prophets' (Matthew 7:12, NIV).

Excellence

Olympic competitors are encouraged to give the best of themselves and progress according to their own objectives. Similarly, the challenge for us in life is not to be better than everyone else, but to better ourselves. We are not in competition with others; we are competing against ourselves, and we should aim to deepen our faith and improve our characters.

For this very reason, make every effort to add to your faith goodness; and to goodness, knowledge; and to knowledge, self-control; and to self-control, perseverance; and to perseverance, godliness; and to godliness, brotherly kindness; and to brotherly kindness, love (2 Peter 1:5–7).

Friendship

The foundation of the Olympics is the bringing together of people from different nations. No one is excluded from the privilege of competing because of the country they are from, the colour of their skin or the language they speak. Likewise, nobody is excluded from the privilege of receiving the grace of God because they are different. Like God, we must accept people from every nation and not allow our differences to become a barrier to friendship. Faith should unify, not divide.

Then Peter began to speak: 'I now realise how true it is that God does not show favouritism but accepts men from every nation who fear him and do what is right' (Acts 10:34–35).

So, winning at all costs is not an Olympic principle and neither is it a biblical principle. The winner does not necessarily take all. It is worth remembering that God's ideas about winning are not our ideas about winning. After all, Jesus was not a winner in the world's eyes when he was crucified with criminals; his victory was in the heavenly realms. Jesus' life offers to us a perfect example of the truth that, in the long term, honour is accorded not to apparent 'winners' but to those who, in the words of the Olympic creed, 'have fought well' in 'the struggle' that is life.

Mark Chester is the founder and chairman of the Who Let The Dads Out? *national initiative, which began in 2003. He currently works full time for Liverpool Football Club as their community family officer.*

Mark is the author of two books, Who Let The Dads Out? *and* School's Out, Dad's About, *both available from www.brfonline.org.uk, or by using the order form on page 153.*

Messy Church and sports

Lucy Moore

'You have no idea how *big* the Olympics are going to be... how they'll *take over* the national consciousness for the whole Olympic season... how *everyone* will be impacted, not just sports fans...'

Some of us hear predictions like this from those who have experienced other Games and rub our hands in glee at the thought of endless sports events to watch and take part in. Others of us groan and slump further down in our sofas, determined to avoid being caught up in any national enthusiasm on principle—especially for sport.

I have to admit I placed myself firmly in the latter camp until I was convinced otherwise by someone who had been in Sydney in 2000 when the Olympics were held there, and waxed lyrical about the opportunities for churches to offer themselves to their village, town or city as a focal point for a local community to join in with a national celebration. Suddenly it made sense to think about the opportunities the Olympics offer rather than the cynical, world-weary (and frankly unChristian) attitude of 'I just can't be bothered...'

With this in mind, the Messy Church team at BRF has produced a short book to help churches make the most of the opportunities for reaching families inspired by the Olympic events in 2012. *Sports Fun for Messy Churches* is full of ideas for churches that want to put on events for communities to enjoy together, regardless of age, ability or disability. If the Olympic organisers are going to be kind enough to provide non-stop publicity and consciousness-raising between now and the end of the Games, and if they are going to do everything possible to help local groups enjoy the event, it surely makes sense to pick up on the wave of awareness and make the most of it in churches.

The Olympics aren't just about sport; they give us a wide range of spiritual themes to explore, which start at a point where people can understand, and have the capacity to lead them into a deeper interest in what the Christian faith has to offer today. These are themes that all sorts of people can enjoy. Competition will appeal to some; an appreciation of different cultures will appeal to others. Healthy lifestyles, discipline, life-coaching, teamwork, excellence, friendship, respect, the idea that coming together to take part in something bigger than our own small lives is a wholesome thing to do... all these themes are starting lines for some sort of spiritual journey for individuals and for families.

Messy Churches are well-placed to be hubs of events, as the Messy Church team is already skilled in thinking about the needs of those outside the established church, from the very young to the very old, those with jumping beans in their pants and those with severe disabilities, those who are still wary of organised religion and those who are hiding behind their children but hearing God's call in some way. The team already understands how to work together under stressed circumstances and will have a grasp of each other's strengths and weaknesses. Most importantly, the Messy Church has been there before the games and will be there afterwards, with its steady monthly presence gradually building a community of strong relationships, discipleship and witness firmly based within the local church. The Olympic opportunities for churches needn't be a flash in the pan—here today, exhausting everyone with a short spurt of excitement, and then disappearing—but can be part of an ongoing strategy.

... opportunities for churches needn't be a flash in the pan

So check out a Messy Church session on sports and the celebration of Olympic values. Have fun making vuvuzelas, bouncing pingpong balls in paint or making energy-drink cocktails. Imagine how families could learn a Bible verse with accompanying exercises. Redeem some local football chants. Try out new ways to pray that involve jogging on the spot: this book is packed with ideas—some safe, some edgy, some plain bonkers, but all good godly fun.

Let's give families an excuse to spend time together, having fun together, communicating, surprising each other, depending on each other, enjoying each other's company. And let the local church be the motivating force behind the events, so that once the games are over, there is still a community to belong to, and the relationships formed over sports trails, safari meals, family grand prix or global cookathons can continue to flourish and draw people closer to God.

Lucy Moore heads up BRF's Messy Church ministry. For more information, visit www.messychurch.org.uk.

An extract from *Dreaming of Home*

Finding a sense of 'home' is a fundamental human longing. In this book, author Michael Mitton draws on his own experience to consider how we can go about finding our true home within God's eternal kingdom, how to identify the forces within us that hinder the search, and the importance of churches offering a welcoming home to all. The following abridged extract is taken from the Introduction to the book.

If I were allowed to travel in time to any moment of my choice, I know where I would like to go. I would ask to be taken to a hillside, as I imagine it, somewhere on a warm sunny afternoon in first-century Palestine. I have slipped away from work early to join a crowd of others who have gathered because they have heard that there is a rabbi in town who has become well known for his wise words and extraordinary miracles. I imagine myself to be in that place of knowing little of the story of this man and yet having an instinct that tells me I need to listen to him, and listen to him with all I've got and for all I'm worth...

I hear a story I know so well in this present age, and yet in my time travelling I am hearing it as it was told for the first time, and so it is completely new to me. The young rabbi shifts his body and now faces me and catches my eye, only momentarily but enough for me to know that he has noticed me and I am included in this group of people whom he is addressing. Here, in this particular place in this time that I have chosen to visit, he has a story to tell, a story that will be talked about for more than 2000 years after its first telling. And he begins, 'There was a man who had two sons...'

... The parables of Jesus must have been extraordinarily powerful when they were first delivered by Jesus as he criss-crossed that ancient land, making his pilgrim way to Jerusalem. Yet, despite the passing of time and the very different culture of 21st-century Britain, this parable of the prodigal son is as compelling and contemporary as ever... [It] is one of the best loved and best known of the parables and is a story where the punchline is to do with coming home. When I allow it to speak to me, I find this simple story, more than any other, makes me aware that within my soul there is a yearning to come home, and it is one of the deepest yearnings of my life...

As I write this I find myself remembering a very good friend who died more than ten years ago and whom I still miss greatly. Brother Ramon SSF was a Franciscan hermit who was known and loved by many people. I used to visit him in his little hermitage at Glasshampton monastery, which is set in beautiful Worcestershire fields... The thing I admired about Ramon was that he was one who was indeed at home in himself and I found his to be a most hospitable home.

Sadly, Ramon became ill with a cancer that eventually took him from us. In his last months he moved out of his airy hermitage into a room in the monastery. On one of the last occasions I visited him he was lying in bed and, though ailing in body, he was very strong in his spirit. At one point, during a conversation in which he was trying to help me understand a complicated piece of mystical theology (which took some doing), he paused and, pulling himself up, leaned towards me and said in his deep, lyrical, Welsh voice, 'You see the trouble with you, Michael, is that you have not yet become Michael Mitton', and the echo of that prophetic insight has resounded in my soul ever since. What he was in effect saying was that I was not yet at home in my own heart, and thus had not yet become who I was born to be...

I know I am not alone in the need to become at home in myself. In the six years that I worked in the training department of Derby Diocese I spent many hours in the company of clergy and lay people who were doing their best to serve Christ faithfully in a church and world of persistent pressures and rapid change. From time to time I have seen something of the pain and alienation that lie behind well-developed defences, and I have found myself with that tell-tale lump in the throat when I see those defences give way, betrayed by the watery signs of human fear and trembling, doubt and sorrow. At those moments I can see evidence that my friends are feeling a kind of homesickness and, to use the poignant language of Psalm 137, are struggling to sing the Lord's song in a foreign land...

It is seeing the signs of being far away from home in my own soul, and in the hearts and minds of those with whom I have been working, that has caused me to develop a determination to find out how we can make our way home. In fact, as I've gone on, I have come to believe that finding the way home may be the only way to make sense of a world where we struggle against confusion, forsakenness and deep weariness.

The subject of home sounds straightforward. In fact, it sounds quite interesting but not particularly exciting. Plenty of people have written books with the word 'home' in their titles, so there is nothing new about it. It seems reasonably safe, nothing too contentious, and generally speaking like familiar ground, for we have all come from homes and live in homes. But, as I have explored this subject, I have found that I am on anything but familiar ground and in territory that is certainly not well defined. I thought that the theme of home would conjure up images of family groups resting by firesides on winter evenings, but instead I found that I was in a far more chilling world of head-on encounters with fears and shames and shadow sides and longings, and only by facing these have I found the road home. For myself, the exploration has been far from safe, and yet wonderfully rewarding...

In the following pages I shall look at the meaning of 'home' and the host of feelings associated with that powerful word, and I shall also look at how we can adventure into our own souls, examining ways of becoming more at home in these lives that have been entrusted to us during our time on earth. I am also interested in the notion that church is home, and how for many who feel emotionally and spiritually homeless in our turbulent world this is good news indeed. As you would expect, the book will end with some thoughts about our final home that we call heaven. From time to time I shall go back to Galilee and listen to that story of the father and his sons and try to garner some of the wealth of insights about homecoming contained in that story, which is as alive for us today as it was when it was first told.

There are fiery signs pointing to our homeland all over this world

Finally, I shall do with this book what I have done with two others of mine, and that is to run alongside the main text a fictional story. It is simply another way of getting the message across, though the beauty of stories is that they engage the imagination, and in that way give you more room to explore the themes...

There are fiery signs pointing to our homeland all over this world. Our task is to be on the lookout in the everyday and ordinary stuff of our lives. So pause and pray that God will touch the eyes of your heart so that through these ordinary pages of print, held alongside your unique experience of life, you will find your own piece of holy ground and catch sight of the fire that is a message for you, a waymark to your homeland.

To order a copy of this book, please visit www.brfonline.org.uk, or turn to the order form on page 153.

Recommended reading

The gifts of God are brought to us in familiar ways and surprising ways, but always free of charge. Some are not recognised as good gifts until we look back and see what God has done through them, while others wait for us to receive and embrace them. Three books published this year by BRF—*Simple Gifts*, *Rhythms of Grace* and *Embracing Dusty Detours*—explore the various blessings that can be found when we open ourselves to God's presence in our everyday lives.

Simple Gifts
Kevin Scully

We are familiar with the idea of friendship as a gift, something that bestows blessing on our lives. Hospitality enriches both giver and receiver, while humour is a gift that, used sensitively, can shed a warm light even on a bleak situation. There are other aspects of life that we may take for granted or even actively dislike—aspects such as ignorance, tears, grief and anger.

Drawing on scripture, song, poetry and insights from daily life, Kevin Scully considers different facets of ten such gifts, from the familiar to the unexpected. He shows how each has the potential to be a source of personal wonder and joy and can also draw us closer to God and to one another. *Simple Gifts* is a book that can be read from beginning to end or dipped into for reflection or inspiration.

> *... the potential to be a source of personal wonder and joy*

Kevin Scully is the author of *Into Your Hands* and *Five Impossible Things to Believe Before Christmas* (BRF), *Imperfect Mirrors* (Shoving Leopard), and *Sensing the Passion* and *Women on the Way* (Triangle/SPCK). A former actor and journalist, he was then ordained in the Church of England and is currently the rector of St Matthew's, Bethnal Green, in London's East End.

Rhythms of Grace
Tony Horsfall

Rhythms of Grace emerges from a personal exploration of contemplative spirituality. Coming from an evangelical and charismatic background, Tony Horsfall felt an increasing desire to know God more deeply. At the same time, he felt an increasing dissatisfaction with his own spiritual life, as well as concern at the number of highly qualified and gifted people involved in Christian ministry who experience burn-out.

... people, places, and little glimpses of eternity

In this book he shows how contemplative spirituality, with its emphasis on realising our identity as God's beloved children and on being rather than doing, has vital lessons for us about discovering intimacy with God. It also provides essential insights about building a ministry that is both enjoyable and sustainable.

Tony Horsfall is a freelance trainer and retreat leader, whose work regularly takes him around the world. He has written a number of other books for BRF, including *Mentoring for Spiritual Growth* and *Working from a Place of Rest*, which has been reprinted twice since publication. He also contributes to *New Daylight* Bible reading notes.

Embracing Dusty Detours
Lynne E. Chandler

'I feel at last that I am embracing the present moment of life. I haven't arrived, I'm just resting; resting beside quiet waters that inevitably churn and stir from time to time and turn into strong currents that drag me back into the river of the hectic everyday.'

This book takes you on a quest through the bustling chaos of Middle Eastern city life and the drama of a youth-led revolution to endless stretches of rolling desert sand, and Bible places from the top of Mount Sinai to the shores of Galilee. This quest, along life's dusty detours, is in search of oases of all kinds—people, places, and little glimpses of eternity.

As in her first book, *Embracing a Concrete Desert* (BRF, 2010), Lynne Chandler relates her experiences in a compelling mixture of laughter, tears and raw honesty, using lyrical prose and poems.

To order a copy of any of these books, please visit www.brfonline.org.uk, or *turn to the order form on page 153.*

SUPPORTING BRF'S MINISTRY

As a Christian charity, BRF is involved in five distinct yet complementary areas.

- **BRF** (www.brf.org.uk) resources adults for their spiritual journey through Bible reading notes, books, and a programme of quiet days and teaching days. BRF also provides the infrastructure that supports our other four specialist ministries.
- **Foundations21** (www.foundations21.org.uk) provides flexible and innovative ways for individuals and groups to explore their Christian faith and discipleship through a multimedia internet-based resource.
- **Messy Church** (www.messychurch.org.uk), led by Lucy Moore, enables churches all over the UK (and increasingly abroad) to reach children and adults beyond the fringes of the church .
- **Barnabas in Churches** (www.barnabasinchurches.org.uk) helps churches to support, resource and develop their children's ministry with the under-11s more effectively .
- **Barnabas in Schools** (www.barnabasinschools.org.uk) enables primary school children and teachers to explore Christianity creatively and bring the Bible alive within RE and Collective Worship.

At the heart of BRF's ministry is a desire to equip adults and children for Christian living—helping them to read and understand the Bible, to explore prayer and to grow as disciples of Jesus. We need your help to make a real impact on the local church, local schools and the wider community.

- You could support BRF's ministry with a donation or standing order (using the response form overleaf).
- You could consider making a bequest to BRF in your will.
- You could encourage your church to support BRF as part of your church's giving to home mission—perhaps focusing on a specific area of our ministry, or a particular member of our Barnabas team.
- Most important of all, you could support BRF with your prayers.

If you would like to discuss how a specific gift or bequest could be used in the development of our ministry, please phone 01865 319700 or email enquiries@brf.org.uk.

Whatever you can do or give, we thank you for your support.

BRF MINISTRY APPEAL RESPONSE FORM

Name ____
Address ____
_________________________________ Postcode ____________
Telephone ____________________ Email _______________________

Gift Aid Declaration

❏ I am a UK taxpayer. I want BRF to treat as Gift Aid Donations all donations I make from 6 April 2000 until I notify you otherwise.

Signature _________________________________ Date ____________

❏ I would like to support BRF's ministry with a regular donation by standing order

Standing Order – Banker's Order

To the Manager, Name of Bank/Building Society
Address ____
_________________________________ Postcode ____________
Sort Code ____________________ Account Name ____________________
Account No ____

Please pay Royal Bank of Scotland plc, Drummonds, 49 Charing Cross, London SW1A 2DX (Sort Code 16-00-38), for the account of BRF A/C No. 00774151

The sum of ______ pounds on ___ / ___ / ___ (insert date) and thereafter the same amount on the same day of each month annually until further notice.

Signature _________________________________ Date ____________

Single donation

❏ I enclose my cheque/credit card/Switch card details for a donation of
£5 £10 £25 £50 £100 £250 (other) £ ______ to support BRF's ministry

Card no. ☐☐☐☐☐☐☐☐☐☐☐☐☐☐☐☐

Expires ☐☐☐☐ **Security code** ☐☐☐ **Issue no.** ☐☐☐☐

Signature _________________________________ Date ____________

Please use my donation for ❏ BRF ❏ Foundations21 ❏ Messy Church
❏ Barnabas in Churches ❏ Barnabas in Schools

❏ Please send me information about making a bequest to BRF in my will.

Please detach and send this completed form to: Richard Fisher, BRF, 15 The Chambers, Vineyard, Abingdon OX14 3FE. BRF is a Registered Charity (No.233280)

BRF PUBLICATIONS ORDER FORM

Please ensure that you complete and send off both sides of this order form.

Please send me the following book(s):

		Quantity	Price	Total
017 2	Whole Life, Whole Bible *(A. Billington)*	______	£6.99	______
877 5	The Way Home *(M. Mitton)*	______	£7.99	______
851 5	Simple Gifts *(K. Scully)*	______	£6.99	______
842 3	Rhythms of Grace *(T. Horsfall)*	______	£7.99	______
829 4	Embracing Dusty Detours *(L.E. Chandler)*	______	£6.99	______
885 0	Who Let The Dads Out? *(M. Chester)*	______	£6.99	______
886 7	School's Out, Dad's About *(M. Chester)*	______	£6.99	______
824 9	Sports Fun for Messy Churches *(L. Moore)*	______	£5.99	______
080 6	The Toddler Bible *(B. James)*	______	£6.99	______
079 0	My First Bible *(L. Lane)*	______	£6.99	______
081 3	The Barnabas Children's Bible *(R. Davies)*	______	£12.99	______

Total cost of books £ ________

Donation £ ________

Postage and packing £ ________

TOTAL £ ________

POSTAGE AND PACKING CHARGES				
order value	UK	Europe	Surface	Air Mail
£7.00 & under	£1.25	£3.00	£3.50	£5.50
£7.01–£30.00	£2.25	£5.50	£6.50	£10.00
Over £30.00	free	prices on request		

For more information about new books and special offers, visit www.brfonline.org.uk.

See over for payment details.

All prices are correct at time of going to press, are subject to the prevailing rate of VAT and may be subject to change without prior warning.

PAYMENT DETAILS

WAYS TO ORDER BRF RESOURCES

Christian bookshops: All good Christian bookshops stock BRF publications. For your nearest stockist, please contact BRF.

Telephone: The BRF office is open between 09.15 and 17.30. To place your order, phone 01865 319700; fax 01865 319701.

Web: Visit www.brfonline.org.uk

By post: Please complete the payment details below and send with appropriate payment and completed order form to:

BRF, 15 The Chambers, Vineyard, Abingdon OX14 3FE

Name ______________________________

Address ______________________________

______________________________ Postcode ____________

Telephone ______________________________

Email ______________________________

Total enclosed £ ____________ (cheques should be made payable to 'BRF')

Please charge my Visa ❑ Mastercard ❑ Switch card ❑ with £ ________

Card no: ☐☐☐☐☐☐☐☐☐☐☐☐☐☐☐☐

Expires ☐☐☐☐ **Security code** ☐☐☐

Issue no (Switch only) ☐☐☐☐

Signature (essential if paying by credit/Switch) ______________________________

❑ Please do not send me further information about BRF publications.

BRF is a Registered Charity

BIBLE READING RESOURCES PACK

Thank you for reading BRF Bible reading notes. BRF has been producing a variety of Bible reading notes for over 90 years, helping people all over the UK and the world connect with the Bible on a personal level every day.

Could you help us find other people who would enjoy our notes?

We produce a Bible Reading Resource Pack for church groups to use to encourage regular Bible reading.

This FREE pack contains:

- Samples of all BRF Bible reading notes.
- Our Resources for Personal Bible Reading catalogue, providing all you need to know about our Bible reading notes.
- A ready-to-use church magazine feature about BRF notes.
- Ready-made sermon and all-age service ideas to help your church into the Bible (ideal for Bible Sunday events).
- And much more!

How to order your FREE pack:

- Visit: www.biblereadingnotes.org.uk/request-a-bible-reading-resources-pack/
- Telephone: 01865 319700
- Post: Complete the form below and post to: Bible Reading Resource Pack, BRF, 15 The Chambers, Vineyard, Abingdon, OX14 3FE

Name ____

Address ______________________________________

____

____________________________ Postcode __________

Telephone _____________________________________

Email ____

Please send me ________ Bible Reading Resources Pack(s)

This pack is produced free of charge for all UK addresses but, if you wish to offer a donation towards our costs, this would be appreciated. If you require a pack to be sent outside of the UK, please contact us for details of postage and packing charges. Tel: +44 1865 319700. Thank you.

BRF is a Registered Charity

NEW DAYLIGHT INDIVIDUAL SUBSCRIPTIONS

❑ I would like to take out a subscription myself:

Your name ______________________________
Your address ______________________________
______________________________ Postcode __________
Tel ______________ Email ______________________

Please send *New Daylight* beginning with the September 2012 / January 2013 / May 2013 issue: (delete as applicable)

(please tick box)	UK	SURFACE	AIR MAIL
NEW DAYLIGHT	❑ £15.00	❑ £17.10	❑ £20.25
NEW DAYLIGHT 3-year sub	❑ £37.80		
NEW DAYLIGHT DELUXE	❑ £18.99	❑ £24.60	❑ £31.50
NEW DAYLIGHT daily email only	❑ £12.00 (UK and overseas)		

Please complete the payment details below and send with appropriate payment to: BRF, 15 The Chambers, Vineyard, Abingdon OX14 3FE

Total enclosed £ __________ (cheques should be made payable to 'BRF')

Please charge my Visa ❑ Mastercard ❑ Switch card ❑ with £

Card no: ❑❑❑❑❑❑❑❑❑❑❑❑❑❑❑❑

Expires ❑❑❑❑ Security code ❑❑❑

Issue no (Switch only) ❑❑❑❑

Signature (essential if paying by card) ______________________

To set up a direct debit, please also complete the form on page 159 and send it to BRF with this form.

BRF is a Registered Charity

NEW DAYLIGHT GIFT SUBSCRIPTIONS

❑ I would like to give a gift subscription (please provide both names and addresses:

Your name ______________________________

Your address ______________________________

______________________________ Postcode ____________

Tel ____________ Email ______________________________

Gift subscription name ______________________________

Gift subscription address ______________________________

______________________________ Postcode ____________

Gift message (20 words max. or include your own gift card for the recipient)

____

____

Please send *New Daylight* beginning with the September 2012 / January 2013 / May 2013 issue: (delete as applicable)

(please tick box)	UK	SURFACE	AIR MAIL
NEW DAYLIGHT	❑ £15.00	❑ £17.10	❑ £20.25
NEW DAYLIGHT 3-year sub	❑ £37.80		
NEW DAYLIGHT DELUXE	❑ £18.99	❑ £24.60	❑ £31.50
NEW DAYLIGHT daily email only	❑ £12.00 (UK and overseas)		

Please complete the payment details below and send with appropriate payment to: **BRF, 15 The Chambers, Vineyard, Abingdon OX14 3FE**

Total enclosed £ ____________ (cheques should be made payable to 'BRF')

Please charge my Visa ❑ Mastercard ❑ Switch card ❑ with £

Card no: ☐☐☐☐☐☐☐☐☐☐☐☐☐☐☐☐

Expires ☐☐☐☐ **Security code** ☐☐☐

Issue no (Switch only) ☐☐☐☐

Signature (essential if paying by card) ______________________________

To set up a direct debit, please also complete the form on page 159 and send it to BRF with this form.

Now you can pay for your annual subscription to BRF notes using Direct Debit. You need only give your bank details once, and the payment is made automatically every year until you cancel it. If you would like to pay by Direct Debit, please use the form opposite, entering your BRF account number under 'Reference'.

You are fully covered by the Direct Debit Guarantee:

The Direct Debit Guarantee

- This Guarantee is offered by all banks and building societies that accept instructions to pay Direct Debits.
- If there are any changes to the amount, date or frequency of your Direct Debit, The Bible Reading Fellowship will notify you 10 working days in advance of your account being debited or as otherwise agreed. If you request The Bible Reading Fellowship to collect a payment, confirmation of the amount and date will be given to you at the time of the request.
- If an error is made in the payment of your Direct Debit, by The Bible Reading Fellowship or your bank or building society, you are entitled to a full and immediate refund of the amount paid from your bank or building society.
  - – If you receive a refund you are not entitled to, you must pay it back when The Bible Reading Fellowship asks you to.
- You can cancel a Direct Debit at any time by simply contacting your bank or building society. Written confirmation may be required. Please also notify us.

The Bible Reading Fellowship

DIRECT Debit

Instruction to your bank or building society to pay by Direct Debit

Please fill in the whole form using a ballpoint pen and send to The Bible Reading Fellowship, 15 The Chambers, Vineyard, Abingdon OX14 3FE.

Service User Number: | 5 | 5 | 8 | 2 | 2 | 9 |

Name and full postal address of your bank or building society

To: The Manager Bank/Building Society

Address

Postcode

Name(s) of account holder(s)

Branch sort code

Bank/Building Society account number

Reference

Instruction to your Bank/Building Society

Please pay The Bible Reading Fellowship Direct Debits from the account detailed in this instruction, subject to the safeguards assured by the Direct Debit Guarantee.
I understand that this instruction may remain with The Bible Reading Fellowship and, if so, details will be passed electronically to my bank/building society.

Signature(s)

Date

Banks and Building Societies may not accept Direct Debit instructions for some types of account.

This page is intentionally left blank.